# One
# Grateful
# IMMIGRANT

## by Leon Staciokas

**ISBN:** 145156855X
**EAN-13:** 9781451568554

Printed in the United States of America

**Editorial Assistance:** Yeazell Consulting, P.O. Box 383194, Duncanville, TX 75138; info@yeazellconsulting.com
**Cover Design and Interior Formatting:** Carmen Rich; carmenrich@cox.net

# Table of Contents

# Prologue

At various times with friends, relatives and acquaintances, whenever the conversation turned to my life's experiences, I would be urged to write my memoirs. In such circumstances I would explain that my experiences were not much different or more interesting than the other Eastern European refugees who fled the oncoming German-Russian front, knowing full well what awaited them under Russian occupation. Many had experienced living in the Communist "paradise" and instead of remaining in their own countries they chose a refugee-wanderer's life in Western Europe.

My wife, Fran, also occasionally encouraged me to write my autobiography. However, the biggest influence was my Cousin, Marytė Spietinienė, who urged, cajoled and begged me to write my life's experiences.

To write an autobiography is a risky undertaking, especially because of my limited and incomplete notes. While writing these memoirs, I had to rely largely on my memory, some notes, letters and photographs. I tried to be objective and tell it like it was, whether good or bad, although some of the remembrances were painful.

Now, at the end of this undertaking, I am thankful to my wife and my Cousin Marytė and those who encouraged me to write. While writing, I had to remember and mentally live through my life all over again, as if a film were moving slowly during these months of writing.

Now I would like to take this opportunity, albeit belatedly, to thank my Cousin Marytė Spietinienė for promising to review and correct my Lithuanian grammar and syntax since my Lithuanian language studies ended more than sixty years ago. Unfortunately, my beloved Cousin Marytė suddenly passed away in 2001 before she had a chance to review my manuscript. I also would like to thank my wife for spending many hours in correcting the English version.

Some readers may note some inconsistencies or contradictions, for which I apologize in advance, because it is not easy to remember everything precisely after seven decades. To the readers of my memoirs, I beg your indulgence and remain sincerely yours.


Leon Staciokas

# Chapter I

## The Boy from Plutiškės Parish

I was born on January 23, 1928 in the village of Vytautiškės, parish of Simnas, Lithuania. My father, as a founder-volunteer in the Lithuanian Independence war of 1918-1922, received approximately a 20 acre land grant where my parents moved before I was born. That farm was sold when I was about one year old and they bought another, slightly larger farm, in the village of Grigaliūniškės, parish of Plutiškės, district of Marijampolė—so, unfortunately, I have no memories of my birthplace. My mother later told me that they did not like living where I was born because the land was poor and they were far away from their relatives.

As a result, I spent my youth in Plutiškės parish.

## *Goose Meat Every Day!*

My first clear memories as a child are associated with the economic crisis in Lithuania beginning in 1933. I remember that the government encouraged my parents and other farmers in our neighborhood to raise geese. They had an agreement with Germany for large quantities of geese sales and all farmers were looking for a way to make a good cash profit. Even though I was still a child, I was old enough to watch over my parent's flocks of geese.

It was a boring task just sitting close to the geese hour after hour. To pass the time I learned the alphabet and with mother's help learned to read, write and count up to a thousand. It was my first love of books that remains with me to this day.

Regrettably, the expected profits from the geese did not materialize. At that time, the Klaipėda region had a large minority of Germans, some of whom advocated incorporating the Klaipėda region with German East Prussia by force. Two leaders, Saass and Neumann, were caught, tried for treason and sentenced to long prison terms. The Germans got mad and canceled the geese purchase agreement. The Lithuanian government was in a bind; the farmers who were encouraged to raise geese now were blaming the government, which had to deal with the excess geese.

To deal with the problem, the government promulgated a very interesting law: all government employees had to buy geese according to their salaries. Farmers were issued coupons according to the number of geese they had for sale and they in turn gave the coupons to the purchasers, one coupon for one goose. The price for geese was fixed by the government. Some, who were highly paid, like my Uncle Leon Gustaitis, a colonel in the Lithuanian army, was obligated to buy more geese than his family could possibly consume. If they did not purchase the designated number of geese, proof of which was possession of coupons, they could not get their next month's salary. The Lithuanian armed forces also were fed geese for months.

Of course, my family also had to consume a large number of geese. I remember my mother making all sorts of meals based on goose meat. Actually, I liked the goose meat and thought it was some kind of a long holiday. In fact, to this day I like goose meat. Most important to me then was that sold or consumed geese did not have to be watched!

### *The Uncles, Cousins and Aunts*

My life was actually quite interesting considering the times. We had no radio, no television and cars were only for the very wealthy who resided primarily in the cities. In the summer my friends and I would climb trees, going from the branch of one tree to the branch of another watching which could go the farthest without touching the ground. Even though we sometimes fell out of a tree, I don't remember any serious injuries. We also went looking for bird nests in the forest or tried to find wild bees "hovels" and appropriate their honey. Of course, one had to be careful not to get stung, which happened sometimes. We also had a small creek where we went swimming, even though the water was only about six-inches deep. Sometimes I had to play with my relatives, when their parents visited us.

I remember one time when my Cousin Marytė and her mother visited us. My mother sent me outside to play with Marytė and I suggested I give her a ride in a wheel barrow. I pushed her for a little while then I got tired. She wanted to ride more, so I dumped her in a puddle of water. She started crying, but I explained to her that the horse got spooked and tipped the wagon over. She believed me, but I am not sure that my aunt and my mother believed me.

My Uncles Gustaitis would sometimes go to the river Jiesia fishing and swimming. I would go with them and that is where I learned to swim and jump from the branches of trees somersaulting into the water.

Visits to my relatives were always welcome. It did not matter if it was Gustaitis, Staciokas, Naginionis or any other relatives. It was a practical matter. While visiting I would get some tasty morsels to eat and occasionally some money, for which I did not have to give account to my mother. On rare occasions there were relatives' weddings. When Uncle Klemensas Gustaitis got married there were all kinds of food including torte. I ate more than I should, except torte, which I did not like. My Aunt Albina's wedding was exciting because the men had a fight. My father was the arbitrator. I believe he was successful because no one got hurt badly. Aunt Ona's wedding was interesting, because to me her husband Raulinaitis was dour and looked like he was mad at the world. I was afraid of him. Afterwards, when I got to know him, we became friends. The only problem was that they lived far from our house and it would take my mother and me half a day walking to get there and back.

One more event that still is in my memory was my journey to visit Uncle Leon Gustaitis in the city of Ukmergė. Before Uncle Leon came over, my mother gave me a bath. I put on the nicest clothes I had and the only pair of shoes that I had. Uncle Leon finally came in a car. All the neighbors ran to the road to see the car, because in the villages at that time a car was a rare event. When I finally got inside the car I did not know how to behave. The seats were so plush and soft, I felt I could sit there for the rest of my life. This was my first ride in a car.

When we arrived to Ukmergė I received a surprise. In the evening my aunt told me to wash my feet before going to bed. I politely explained to her that I had a bath that morning and since I did not remove my shoes all day, my feet certainly were quite clean. She informed me that I would have to wash my feet every night before going to bed. Those couple of weeks passed rather fast and I had a great time. When I came home, I explained to mother that I should be washing my feet every night like my aunt told me. I do not remember how that all ended; probably in a few days I forgot all about it.

Another astonishing event in my young life happened in the summer of 1937 when my Aunt Kukanskis and my Cousin Peter came for a visit from the United States. They stayed with us. I know that my parents' farm work suffered because we were using the horses to take them around to visit other relatives. Wherever they went I was their constant companion. I ate a lot of ice cream since Cousin Peter paid for it. He always invited me to be with him, except when he visited our neighbor's daughter. In those occasions he would tell me in no uncertain terms that I was not welcome.

In the winter we would go skating on ours' or our neighbor's pond. The skating was quite a complicated affair. The skate, only on one foot, was made from a discarded scythe that was hammered into a wooden shoe. One had to be careful not to splinter the wooden shoe putting the skate in and taking it out.

## *Escape from My Mother's Skirt*

Another important event in my young life was connected with the church. On Sundays we and our neighbors would go to the Plutiškės church services. Women would walk barefooted and put on their shoes near the church, while the men would wear their shoes all the way from home to the church. We children had to go with our barefoot mothers and put our shoes on near the church. In church the men were on the right while women and children (including boys until about 13 years of age) would go to the left side of the church.

At age six or seven, I did not want to be with mother and the other women until I was 13 years old, at which time I could go with father. In my mind, six or seven more years were like an eternity. Although I did not like sitting with mother, I did not object, which would have been totally unacceptable and I might even have gotten punished for such "heresy". I reasoned that there had to be a way to detach myself from my mother's skirt. Finally I got the idea that if I became an altar boy I would not have to spend church services with the "old women". Of course, one had to learn Roman Catholic Church services in Latin, but to my thinking, that was a small price for my freedom.

I volunteered to be an altar boy to priest Steponaitis and he agreed to teach me the services in Latin. I told my parents about the good news, not revealing the real reason for my devotion to religion. I also bragged to my grandmother Staciokas knowing that she would speak favorably, because she always said that when I grew up I should become a priest. Everyone agreed. Now all I had to do was commit myself to learn Latin.

After a few months I passed father Steponaitis' test and we went to see pastor Ilgūnas. As it was customary, before speaking, I kissed the pastor's hand. Father Steponaitis stated that I knew all the church rites in Latin. After the pastor was satisfied, he told father Steponaitis to make arrangements for me to serve as altar boy the following Sunday. I was overjoyed. I am not sure if it was because I was able to serve mass or that I did not have to be with mother and other women during church services. I must confess that the church services were to my liking. I was an altar boy not only in Plutiškės and Veiveriai, but after the war, in the POW camp whenever there was a catholic priest available.

When we were released from the POW camp and settled in Germany, I was not only serving mass to the Lithuanian chaplain, but was overseeing all the necessary affairs of the chapel, i.e. made sure that the church clothes were in order, that we had sacrament wine and that the chapel was in good order and clean. Effectively I was the sacristan for the Lithuanian chaplain. Of course, this was free-gratis because I had another job, which I will describe later.

### Sorrows

Although in my youth I had wonderful and joyous experiences, the sorrows of life did not pass me by. Around May of 1941 the Russians collected many men, among them my Uncles Alfonsas and Juozas Gustaitis, to dig antitank ditches at the Russian-German border. A few days after the start of the German-Russian war on June 22, 1941 and after the Germans swept past our area, the men began to return. Uncle Juozas came back with other men. We waited about a week or more, but Uncle Alfonsas and three of his relatives and friends had not returned. My father, Uncle Naginionis and Uncle Gustaitis began to inquire about the four men.

About a month later we finally received news that near the city of Marijampolė the Germans had shot four men and maybe they were the men that we were looking for. My father, Uncle Gustaitis and Uncle Naginionis went to the described area and found four men buried, among them my Uncle Alfonsas. They were reburied with great ceremony at the Plutiškės church, in services conducted by three priests. With tears in my eyes, I was the altar boy in these ceremonies. There were big crowds during the ceremonies that extended from the church to the cemetery, about half a mile distance. My mother and Aunt Albina cried and it was impossible to console them. They had to be restrained by my father and Uncle Naginionis.

One more painful event was the arrest of my Uncle Leonas Gustaitis in December of 1940. We could not get any information about his situation, where was he, the charges against him, was he well, etc. The Communist authorities proclaimed they knew nothing about him even to his wife. After the front passed Lithuania into Russia, we found out that for a while my Uncle Leonas was in Riga, Latvia in prison. About June 25 he was transported to Russia where he disappeared without a trace. When I visited Lithuania in 1972, my Aunt Ona, his wife, visited me in Vilnius and told me that Uncle Leonas was shot somewhere in Bielorussia. When I saw my mother for the last time, she gave me Uncle Leonas' picture when he was in prison. I will value this picture for the rest of my life.

Oh what beautiful plans were made in my family in the third decade of that century. Uncle Leonas Gustaitis, while I was still in grammar school, promised to take me to live with him after I graduated from gymnasium and would make sure that I obtained a university education. Afterwards, I would go to military school, become an officer and live a military life. It was, even for me, difficult to believe about the "heaven" that was to be mine in the future. However, all the plans, wishes and expectations vanished so quickly and so brutally. Instead, the reality was that the Second World War began in 1939, Russia occupied Lithuania in 1940 and again in 1945, my Uncle Leonas was arrested and murdered, the German occupation of 1941-1945, my Uncle Alfonsas was murdered by Germans and untold suffering of my relatives under

11

the Russian and German occupations. As for me, like a forgotten wanderer, after bouncing all over Europe, I finally settled in the United States.

## *School Days*

During my years living in Lithuania the school system consisted of primary (grammar) school – four years (mandatory); gymnasium – eight years (academically competitive and tuition based) and; university – four years (academically competitive and tuition based). My first two years in grammar school were spent in a one-room schoolhouse. Around 1935, Plutiškės built a new school, which is now a part of a much larger school housing 12 grades. In the thirties and until after the war, Plutiškės had only four grades. At that time the mandatory education in Lithuania was only four years.

From the first day in school I was bored. I complained to my mother and upon her advice, I asked teacher Valaitis to promote me to the second grade since I already knew how to read and write and count up to a thousand. After satisfying the teacher's examination, he promoted me to the second grade and assigned me a seat next to the father of the current principal of the Plutiškės high school.

I completed four years of grammar school

in only three years. Since Plutiškės did not have any more grades, I went to Šilavotas, where there were fifth and sixth grades, or effectively the first and second year of gymnasium. After studying for one year and with the help of teacher Rimaitis, I passed two grades and on the first of September, 1937 I was accepted to the third year of Veiveriai gymnasium.

While attending grammar school in Plutiškės, I was not only an altar boy in church, but I also engaged in some "business" deals. A nice Jewish fellow by the name of Velpkė had a general store in Plutiškės. He also had an invalid daughter that was going to the same grammar school with me. One day her father asked me if I would help her to cross a little narrow bridge. For my assistance he promised me some candy. However, not wishing that my friends would tease me for holding hands with an invalid Jewish girl, as I had promised her father, I made her cross that bridge by herself with me going backwards ahead of her. I also threatened her if she told her father that I was not holding her hand while crossing the bridge. At any rate, I got candy almost all year. That episode was not one of the better examples of my behavior—it was my youthful stupidity.

Looking through my eyes, Velpkė's store had everything. The problem was I did not have the money to buy things I wanted, especially exploding corks. One day I figured out how to make money. My mother boiled two eggs for lunch in school; I cooled and sold them to Velpkė's wife as fresh eggs. With half of the money I bought a herring and with the rest of the money bought exploding corks. For a couple weeks I heard nothing, so I figured I could make a little money with some more boiled eggs.

One evening my father came back from a farmer's market and said he wanted to tell something to my mother, but insisted that I hear what he had to say. Father said that he met Velpkė at the market and he told my father that his son Leon will be a good businessman, because he sold his wife boiled eggs as fresh. Father reprimanded me for dishonesty and at the same time laughed at my "cleverness"; so ended my "business" with boiled eggs.

One time my mother sent me to buy a pound of sugar. While carrying the sugar home I "sampled" some of it. When I brought it in the house, my mother remarked that it looked very small for a pound. I told her that I squeezed the bag very hard and that is why it looked so small. Of course, she did not believe me and demanded the truth. I finally confessed and avoided punishment.

Sometimes when I did not have money and

wanted to buy something, I would borrow money from other children. The problem was I could not repay them, so they complained to the teacher. He in turn invited my father for a "consultation". Father had to repay the loans to the kids and when I came home, there was a belt waiting for me; so ended my desire to go in debt.

## *Gymnasium, University, Stalin, Lenin and the War*

I was overjoyed when I was accepted and became a third year student in gymnasium. I was very proud of the uniform I had to wear, particularly on Sundays in church. As I remember, my parents were also proud, although they had to somehow scrape up the money for the uniform. We traveled to Marijampolė to a real city tailor, who measured me and tailored the uniform. My father's brother was a tailor and always tailored our clothes, but in my judgment, he was not a "city tailor" that could make uniforms. I regret that I never said anything to my uncle and never apologized. This is another time where youth's false pride overruled good judgment.

The year 1938 was the twentieth anniversary of Lithuanian independence. That summer I was tutoring my neighbor's son and at the same time I was also studying. That fall I passed the required exams and was promoted to the fifth year of the eight year gymnasium. To me the studies came relatively easy and by September 1939, I skipped another grade and became a seventh year student. That was the day when Germany attacked Poland and it was the beginning of the Second World War.

Initially we knew nothing of war's destruction or Stalin's and Hitler's agreements that divided Poland and the Baltic States amongst themselves—they were distant and unfathomable events that had no affect on me, or so I thought then. However, everything changed very quickly. The Russians offered the Lithuanians an unfavorable agreement, which Lithuania, being a small country, was in no condition to reject.

I remember various discussions among students and teachers. The majority opinion was that it would not be so bad for Lithuania; after all, we were able to reclaim the Vilnius region, which for 20 years was occupied by Poland. What naïve thinking from most of the people! Then we were not familiar with the Communist system and had no idea about Stalin's governing methods, which later we had to experience with much regret.

On June 15, 1940 our school year ended and I, being promoted to the final (eighth) year of gymnasium, cheerfully left for home and summer vacation. September of 1940 was a very different first day of school compared to the previous years. The first thing that was different was that we had to attend an all students meeting with big pictures of Stalin and Lenin and huge propaganda slogans paraded throughout the meeting. Most of us refused to carry these placards.

We were also told that religion classes were stopped and instead we would study Stalin's constitution. The nine o'clock student mass on Sundays was no longer a part of the student requirements. In fact, the students were discouraged from going to church. But what really happened was the opposite. I remember, when in earlier times, our homeroom teachers encouraged us to go to church on Sunday for student mass. One should remember that Lithuania was over 80% catholic.

On Mondays we found all sorts of reasons why we did not attend church on Sunday: "I was not feeling good, I had a lot of homework, I went home that weekend, etc." After the first meeting and the "advise" of the teachers, the following Sunday at nine o'clock mass in Veiveriai church was full of students. This was the first open opposition to the occupiers. Most of the teachers were neutral and did what they were ordered to do, however, without enthusiasm. We found many new teachers had replaced the old. Some of them tried to explain to us the virtues of communism, but most of us paid no attention to their "preaching".

I remember when I was called to explain why, for a couple of weeks, I was in church serving as altar boy. I explained that my deeply religious grandmother wanted me to do that. That time I got away with it, however, a bigger problem later arose. In 1941, Easter fell on April 13 and that Easter Sunday we had to attend classes, according to the "*ukaz*," (Russian word for order), which would substitute for the day off on May first (a big Communist holiday).

Shortly before Palm Sunday, I went to the doctor complaining that I had a sore knee due to a fall while playing basketball. The doctor gave me an excuse slip good until April 11. That, of course, did not cover Easter Sunday on the 13th. So I took the "liberty" and changed the date of 11 to 17. Unfortunately, my ink did not quite match the doctor's ink, but I did not notice it. Before leaving for home I met one of the teachers at the bus station and handed her the slip.

On Easter Sunday our family went to church. After the service, a student that I knew handed my father a letter from the principal of the school which stated: "citizen, your son can not return to school without your accompanying him for a conference with me," or something similar. I explained to my father what I had done. He did not scold me, although we were uneasy as to what might happen.

After the 17th my father and I were met by my classroom teacher, Miss Ralkevičiūtė, who was also a Russian language teacher. She explained to my father that I committed a serious crime—I falsified a document. However, considering that I was a good student, I could remain in school, but at the end of the year my behavior grade would be reduced. That meant that I would not be admitted to any Lithuanian university, a big blow to my future plans. In addition, I would not be permitted to join Komsomol (the Communist youth organization) for at least a year or two. I was overjoyed to hear that, although my face did not show my joy. After the meeting neither my father nor I were too happy, but we decided we would wait and see what the future held.

When I was released from the POW camp, I found out that Miss Ralkevičiūtė was living in the same displaced persons camp as my friend's parents. I visited the camp and met Miss Ralkevičiūtė, reminding her about our discussion in the spring of 1941. She laughed and said that I should be thankful because she defended me in the teacher's meeting. I thanked her for that.

I believe that in 1950, when I was living in the

United States, through Lithuanian newspapers, I learned that she came to United States and was living in New London, Connecticut, which was not too far from where I was living, in Waterbury, Connecticut. I went to visit her and this time I bought her a good dinner and that long evening we shared our experiences of the past decade. We corresponded for probably 20 years until she passed away.

Germany attacked the Soviet Union on June 22, 1941. After the Germans swept through Lithuania, I applied to the Polytechnic Institute in Kaunas, explaining why my behavior grade was reduced. There was no problem and I was accepted. The 1941-1944 school years were not very pleasant. There were all kinds of shortages, i.e. food, clothing and other items required for daily living. By the fall of 1942, I decided that I should make some money in the black market. On periodic travels to my parents, I began to bring in to town some bacon and moonshine. I met a man who had a rowboat, and he agreed to transport me and the goods across the Nemunas River. The bridge in Kaunas' suburb was too dangerous to cross because it was heavily patrolled by the police who were looking for black marketers. If caught, one faced heavy penalties, maybe some jail time and later as a forced laborer in Germany.

Sometimes I was successful in finding products in the city that were in great demand in the villages and managed to get them by bartering.

My studies were going very well. In January-March of 1944 I passed some exams, completed laboratory work and was able to take the fourth year mandatory courses. In June 1944 I was allowed to graduate with an electrical engineering degree.

## *Home for the Holidays*

Because all my schools, except Plutiškės, were too far away to walk to on a daily basis, I had to stay in boarding houses, four years in Veiveriai and three years in Kaunas. One year I lived with quasi-nuns in Šilavotas. At that time in Lithuania there were women who did not want to get married and have families. They chose to live by themselves, attend Mass every day and help out with church needs. Most of the women were skilled seamstresses or weavers and would wash church clothing and clean the church. Some of the women were able to live independently on the support they received from an inheritance. They congregated close to church and would take students as boarders, with compensation, of course.

My visits home were only on occasional weekends and vacations. Whenever I went home for the weekend, my father encouraged me to help mother feed the pigs, milk the cows and bring water from the well. After those chores, mother would suggest I go and help father feed and water the animals. That would be my Saturday. On Sunday morning, dad would suggest that I start the wood fire in the stove for breakfast, then we went to church and in the afternoon I was ready to go back to school, mostly walking. Only in Kaunas did I use motorized transport, mostly milk trucks, because during the war there was very little public inter-city transport. The milk truck or other truck drivers would not take money, so bacon or small bottles of moonshine were the "currency".

During the summer months I helped my parents with farm work. Therefore, I learned how to cut hay, harvest crops, plow and rake fields, feed animals and milk cows. I was familiar with manure and fertilizing the fields, and knew how to load and unload wagons with crops and to do all kinds of other farm work.

# Chapter II

## In the Army Now!

In the spring of 1944, the Germans were retreating across the whole Eastern Front and it was just a matter of time before the Russians again occupied Lithuania. My parents understood that life would not be pleasant under the new Russian Communist occupation. We were considering retreating to the West, that is, to Germany. However, we knew that we would not be permitted to cross Germany's border because no one in our family was serving in the German Armed Forces. After many discussions, it was decided that I would join the German Armed Forces so that my parents and other relatives would be permitted to retreat to Germany.

I entered the German Air Force on June 2, 1944, and my mother immediately regretted the decision. She felt that I was too young to enter military service and most likely would not survive the war. Losing her only son, which she was sure would happen, was not to her liking. She even came to the military collection center and tried to persuade the German military authorities to release me—to no avail. I was in uniform and that was that.

On June 15, 1944, already in uniform, I received my degree and continued recruit training. On July 4 we left Lithuania for Germany. The plan was that we would go to Czechoslovakia, (Germans then called it Monrovia/Bohemia protectorate) for a parade and in two weeks return to Lithuania. In the later part of July, while we were preparing for the return trip to Lithuania, the Russians occupied Vilnius and a large part of Lithuania. We were sent to East Prussia, about 35 miles from Konigsberg (present day Kaliningrad) to the Air Force Academy. There, in three months, we completed fighter pilot training including 16 parachute jumps. I received a lieutenant's rank and fighter pilot wings. We were going to be assigned either to the eastern or western part of Germany to defend the German cities from Russian and/or American-British air raid bombings.

During the second week in the academy a

noteworthy event took place not too far away from the academy. This was July 20, 1944, the day that Colonel Von Staufenberg attempted to kill Hitler by leaving a briefcase with a bomb near Hitler's chair in the conference room. Unfortunately, the bomb did not kill Hitler, only injured him. We found out about it a few hours later when the academy commandant spoke to us. It was a strange day: no classes, no flight instructions and no inspection of any kind. We cadets felt no changes other than the fact that within a few days we were prohibited from using an ordinary military salute by raising our hand to the edge of our hat or cap. From that day on we were required to use the Nazi salute. We did not like it, but an order was an order. Amongst ourselves we even used a saying "my dog jumps this high" when raising our hands to do the Nazi salute.

## *Himmler's Decision and the Air Raid Chickens*

At that time the Germans had a very limited number of planes and even less fuel. Our fighter wing was demobilized and we, wearing Air Force uniforms, were sent to Stettin (present day Polish city of Szczecin) for infantry training. After about four weeks, or at the beginning of November, we were transported to the city of Bonn where we spent about three months.

During the infantry training we experienced

a very unpleasant event. One morning we were not being awakened as usual. After a little while we noticed a curious situation. Our building was surrounded by an SS detachment and no one was permitted to leave the building. After about half a day's confinement we received a Lithuanian Colonel Liormanas, dressed in German Air Force colonel's uniform, who informed us that we were being confined to our barracks until Himmler, the chief of the Waffen SS made up his mind what to do with us. Himmler wanted to send us and other Lithuanian units scattered throughout Germany and German occupied territories to concentration camps for treason. Colonel Liormanas told us that he had an audience with Herr Himmler and tried to intercede on our behalf.

What happened was that a battalion of Lithuanians fighting in Italy with Germans against English forces crossed the lines and surrendered to the Polish forces on the Allied side. Evidently Colonel Liormanas visit with Himmler was successful because we were allowed to complete the infantry training and ultimately sent to the Russian front.

Later, while in the POW camp, I found out that the captain who led the Lithuanian forces to the Allies was the brother of Major Gecevicius who was with me in the same POW camp and later was our commandant in the Displaced Persons Camp in Bocholt, Westphalia where I spent over three years. In the Displaced Persons Camp he was very helpful to me by offering to teach me how to type, and recommended me as a typist in the British office: British Control Commission for Germany. (My experiences in the BCCG is described somewhere else in this book.)

During this time, Cologne and Bonn were heavily bombed and we were required to go to the cities to help extinguish fires and search for people in the bombed-out building. One night, just shortly before the New Year during one of the air raids, our barracks were also destroyed. In this fire, I lost all my personal possessions such as photographs, my diploma, birth certificate and other articles dear to me.

It is well known that the Germans were very diligent to register everything—for example, the people living in the cities that had chickens had to register the number of chickens. One day, while trying to save furniture and other goods from the burning houses, a young German girl approached our captain and asked if he had anybody that could kill and clean a few chickens. For their assistance the captain and the "butcher" would get a chicken each. Being close by, I overheard the conversation and offered to help. I killed six or eight chickens, cleaned and cut them up. As promised, the captain and I, each received a butchered chicken. That evening, we had a food feast because the food for the soldiers away from the front lines was not the best. That young lady surely notified the authorities that the chickens disappeared during the bombing raid. In my mind, I thanked my parents for teaching me fundamental survival skills, that is, food preparation.

### British Prisoner of War

In time our former Air Force group was divided: some men were assigned to the anti aircraft batteries to defend against dive bomber attacks of Rhine River shipping, while others including me were sent to the outskirts of Hamburg for the formation of a new division, which was to be sent to the Russian front. At the beginning of March, I found myself about 35 miles north west of Berlin in the Russian front. We were retreating—sometimes orderly, sometimes disorderly. Near Lubeck our company fell apart, as I and several other Lithuanians retreated towards Denmark. It was May 2, 1945.

Upon noticing tanks with white five-corner stars we hid in the bushes, deciding not to surrender to the Russians. A little later, when the soldiers stuck their heads out of the top of the turrets, it became clear that these were not Russians but

English. (In those days the American tanks with white five corner stars—American insignia—were sent to the allies, and the Russians being allies were immediately dispatched to the front without repainting them with the respective country insignias). Once we recognized that the soldiers were English we rushed to surrender. We knew that the Russians were not far from there.

What can one say about the life in a Prisoner of War camp? POW, irrespective of the country, is a restriction of human activity; one has no name, only a number. You are behind barbered wire being guarded by a foreign military. POW's and prison inmates' lives are similar, the difference is that an inmate, who was sentenced in court for a crime against society, knows how long he/she will be in prison, while a prisoner of war, taken by an opposing military, does not know when the release will take place.

When one compares the Russian POW— to which I was determined not to surrender because I had heard about life there—with the British POW; I was quite happy to surrender to the British. Sometime in 1959, after Stalin "kicked the bucket" on March 5, 1953, we found out that out of half a million Germans and their allies in the Russian POW camps, only about five thousand came back alive in 1955. By the way, this number does not include the Japanese that fell into Russian hands when the Russians declared war against Japan three weeks before the end of hostilities between Japan and the United States and its allies in the Pacific. I have read somewhere that from about one million Japanese soldiers that were in Russian POW camps, after 10 years, only about 10% came home.

Our first two months in the British POW camps were spent in the Kiel area of the Schleswig-Holstein region in Northern Germany which was surrounded by the British military. But, inside this perimeter we were virtually unguarded. Slowly, in about a month, we Lithuanians were collected together into a Lithuanian "battalion" of about 2,000 men. We dug holes in the ground, covered them with tree branches—our "bedrooms"—and waited, not knowing what the future would bring. There were rumors that the American/British alliance would form Lithuanian and other Baltic States divisions in preparation for war with the Soviet Union.

At the beginning of July, we were collected in the nearest railroad station and virtually without guards, traveled southwest. After a few hours we entered Holland traveling south, accompanied by threats with pitchforks by the Dutch farmers who assumed we were Germans, since we wore

German uniforms. Thank God, the train never stopped. After a while, we entered Belgium traveling west. Finally, the train stopped near a camp surrounded by barbered-wire fences. It looked strange that future soldiers of the allies would wind up behind barbered-wire fence. Through the loudspeakers we received command to leave the train. We did not know then that this would be our POW camp for the next year.

The rules were explained very simply: Belgian soldiers would be guards while the British would have the administrative responsibility. If anyone crossed the marked "death" ditch, which was about six feet from the barbered-wire fence, they would be shot without warning.

Life in the POW camp was not too bad. Nobody harmed us physically or mentally. We only had two problems: 1) Inadequate food, which resulted in constant hunger, and 2) British, observing the Geneva Convention for prisoners of war, would not allow us to work other than to maintain order within the camp. Consequently, boredom and hunger were our daily companions. Having a lot of free time, I learned how to play respectable chess. In April 1946, we were released from the POW camp.

While in the POW camp I met one of our neighbors from Lithuania. We talked about our country and our homes. This is when I learned the sad truth that my parents were unable to retreat to Germany. He described to me how he and his battalion were retreating towards our village and on the way stopped at my parents' house. There was Uncle Klemensas Gustaitis with his family and my parents with horses hitched to the wagons and loaded with goods ready to travel towards Germany. He wished them good travel and went to his house. While eating, his brother ran into the house telling him that the Russians were only about a mile away, going through Staciokas' and other neighbors' lands. His brother suggested that he grab a horse and try to catch up with his troops. Luckily, after a few miles, he caught up with his battalion. There were some light fights, but he successfully retreated towards Germany.

I was very upset for a while since my plans to help my parents escape communism went by the wayside. Personally I was satisfied that, at least presently, I would not have to live under the Communist occupation. We, of course, hoped to be back in Lithuania after a year or less. At that time we did not know that the American-British alliance had turned over to Stalin Eastern Europe and part of Germany—for free, even adding large amounts of war materials to the deal.

While in POW camp, we were visited by the

Soviet propaganda "orators," NKVD, later known as the KGB. They were dressed in Soviet military uniforms, urging us to go back to our home countries. In our camp we had about 10,000 Latvians, about 1,500 Estonians and about 2,000 Lithuanians. We were tempted to kill the Russians, but the camp commandant told us not to provoke them and create an incident against an "ally" and cause difficulties for him. As a gesture to show how much we wanted to go to the Soviet "paradise," when the Russian officer started talking, instead of facing him, we turned our backs and dropped our pants. He threatened that we would remain there until we died. Our representatives told the Russians that we would rather die there than in Siberia, thus ended the Russians urging us to return to our countries. Out of about 13,500 Baltic soldiers in that POW camp only five agreed to return. Later we established that two were Communist spies and three were camp thieves that previously had been punished by fellow POW's.

# Chapter III

## After the War

Early in April 1946, we were released from the POW camp and allowed to choose where we wanted to live—limited to the Baltic States or Germany. Without exception, we all chose Germany. We were housed in a former Russian POW camp and a status as Displaced Persons or abbreviated DP. We began calling ourselves *"GOD'S BIRDS"* (in Lithuanian: **"D**ievo **P**aukšteliai," a take-off from the DP initials). This was our first exposure to diplomacy between the American and British democracies and the Soviet Communist dictatorship. In reality, we were not DISPLACED PERSONS but REFUGEES from the brutal Soviet

Communist dictatorship.

Such diplomacy between the war allies took place before the start of the Cold War and Churchill's famous speech at Fulton, Missouri, where he coined the term "Iron Curtain". The name Displaced Persons was given to all refugees in the Western European countries. In Germany alone there were several million refugees. The refugee camps were divided along nationality lines. Hence, there were Lithuanian, Latvian, Estonian, Polish, Ukrainian, Yugoslavian and, of course, German refugee camps. The German refugees were from East Prussia, German lands incorporated into Poland and the eastern part of Germany that was occupied by the Soviet Union. There were also Jewish camps consisting of the Jews that survived the holocaust and the concentration camp horrors.

The life for Germans was very difficult because Germany, particularly German cities, were utterly destroyed. The life for the refugees of other nationalities was especially hard, even though the United Nations Relief Organization was responsible for them. The Relief Organization administration, consisting mostly of poorly educated "allies" and Soviet sympathizers, was corrupt and ridden with thievery which resulted in reduced rations, inadequate housing and poor health provisions. The life for refugees slowly improved when people began to find work and improve their well being. Some became "business people" engaged in the black market. In all fairness, in time, some of the incompetents and crooks in the UN Relief Organization were eventually weeded out. Because of the shortages, the black market flourished with cigarettes and coffee beans as currency, since the Reichsmark was worthless due to inflation.

Our camp was different from other Lithuanian refugee camps. We were all men, former POW's, while other camps contained families, unmarried men who were not soldiers and women. As soon as we settled we needed camp administration. It was discovered that no one out of 2,000 individuals in the camp knew how to use a typewriter. Major Gecevičius, the Lithuanian camp commandant, asked me if I wanted to learn how to type. I agreed when I found out that the British Administration for the refugee camps were willing to pay for me to learn. In about a month, I became reasonably proficient with the typewriter. At the same time I started to work in the Lithuanian camp administration. My life improved, although the pay I received was in the worthless German money, but the supplemental food and clothing rations were especially significant.

When I had time, I started to learn some English because we had contacts and dealings with the British administration. As I mentioned earlier, I assisted the Lithuanian chaplain as altar boy and worked to insure that the other matters related to the chapel and the chaplain were taken care of.

After working for about a year-and-a-half in the Lithuanian administration, I was invited to work as a typist in the British Control Commission for Germany (BCCG) offices. This organization, among other things, was also responsible for the administration of all displaced persons camps in the British zone of occupation and later Jewish Transit camp for Palestine. Our refugee camp housed over 8,000 refugees. Those of us working in BCCG, one Lithuanian, myself, three Latvians and two Estonians, received scripts with which we could purchase items in the British military stores such as chocolate, cigarettes, coffee beans and other items that were unavailable in the German stores. Life for me improved measurably.

In 1947, when our camp became a Jewish transit camp for Palestine—today's Israel—my work also required me to deal with the Jewish representatives. Our common language with them was German and Russian. I got along very well with the Jewish people and whenever I could I tried to help those that did not have the proper and required documentation. I did that not for profit but for humanitarian reasons. There was a rumor in the Jewish Transit Camp that if there was a need to "fix things up," Staciokas would help. As a result, the local Jewish administration gave me gifts of whiskey or cigarettes and occasionally invited me to dinners.

In 1948, there was a currency reform in Germany. The new Deutschemark replaced the worthless Reichsmark. The best part for me was that within a week after the currency reform, I received my monthly salary in the new currency. What was most astonishing was that almost overnight the stores were full of consumer goods. After getting my first pay in D-marks, I purchased a bicycle, a luxury at that time.

### Lady Liberty on the Horizon

In 1947, Great Britain, Belgium, Canada and Australia began visiting refugee camps looking for workers. Great Britain wanted farm workers, Belgium wanted people to work in the coal mines, and Canada wanted forest and gold mine workers, while Australia was looking for general industrial workers. Australia was the only country at that time willing to take families, while others wanted only men with good health.

I was prepared to emigrate to anywhere outside Germany. Although I knew the German language and understood German culture, which was acceptable to me, I did not want to remain in Germany, since I was convinced that I would forever be a second-class citizen. In those days Germans were not at all friendly with foreigners. I corresponded with my relatives in the United States and occasionally received packages or a few dollars. In one of the letters from my Aunt Monica Raškauskas, she wrote that the United States Congress was considering a Refugee Immigration Act and I should be patient. I listened to her and indeed, the Refugee Immigration Act became US law early in 1948 allowing some 300,000 Displaced Persons to immigrate to the United States.

It should be noted, that in 1948 United States began to call us REFUGEES, not Displaced Persons. The Cold War was on and niceties in reference to the Soviet Union were not required, in fact insults were acceptable. As I have noted earlier, the name "Displaced Persons" was created to pacify Soviet objections regarding refugees who were fleeing from the advancing Red Army. One should recognize that there were no fleeing refugees from the advancing American or British armies. In fact, fleeing refugees were trying to reach Western European regions where there was a chance that the Americans or British would overrun that area.

Because I already had an affidavit from Uncle

Kukanskis guaranteeing me a job and living accommodations, I was given priority even though I was living in the British, not American zone of occupation. Of course, I had to pass all sorts of obstacles, such as a health examination, occupation, proof that I was not a Communist, etc. In other words, an elephant could pass through the eye of a needle easier than an immigrant could pass through the requirements of the Immigration and Naturalization Services.

One particular incident stands out in my mind. After I succeeded in passing all health and other requirements in the transit camp, the last stop was the United States Immigration and Naturalization Services Office where the immigration visa would be issued. The INS officer was commenting that my service in the German Air Force was a negative in his mind. He wondered what I would do if I did not get the visa, since my refugee camp would not take me back. My answer was very straight: I told him that I was healthy, alone, young, spoke German fluently and I was certain I would find a job in the German economy. He smiled and said: "we need your kind of people" and stamped my documents giving me the visa: permanent residence in the United States. On July 28 I boarded a Liberty Ship "Gen. Mac Rae" in Bremenhafen, Germany and on August 7, reached New York harbor.

## FINALLY AMERICA!

It was about three o'clock on the morning of August 7th when I awoke to go to work in the ship's kitchen—where I worked the entire journey across the Atlantic Ocean—that I noticed that the ship was not moving. When I got to the deck, I could barely see the Statue of Liberty which was several miles away. Finally at about 8 o'clock, when most of my work in the kitchen was finished, I noticed the ships movement. I went to the deck, which was already crowded with people, and could see the Statue of Liberty not far away. I, along with the crowd, watched as the ship passed the Statue of Liberty and headed for one of the piers with the help of a tugboat. As the ship was finally moored, we all waited to be let out on United States soil. It is impossible to describe the feelings when one is so close to stepping on solid American ground.

I remember, while sailing the Atlantic Ocean, how we talked about arriving in the United States. No one worried or talked about how we were going to make a living or what awaited us in the future; all we talked about was how lucky we were to be going to the United States. Some even wondered if we would be closed in some kind of camp, since it leaked out that there was an Island (Ellis Island) where all potential immigrants where housed for a period of time and the determinations made who would be permitted to enter the United States as permanent residents. As we passed the Statue of Liberty, the loudspeakers announced that we were passing Ellis Island.

We were also told that the former practices at Ellis Island had been abandoned some years prior and that our permission to permanently reside in the United States was determined in the transit camp in Germany. You can imagine what a relief it was to hear those reassuring words that we already had permission to permanently reside in the United States.

When I arrived in the United States my wealth consisted of a handmade wooden suitcase, one suit, two pairs of shoes, one pair of pants, about three sets of underwear, a couple of pairs of socks and ten dollars in my pocket.

## *Easy Beginnings*

My beginning in America was a joy compared to the experience of other immigrants. The first thing that happened on arrival was checking documents and personality verification. For example: the documents of a family consisting of a husband and wife and two children had to match the ship's manifest. At the same time, people were selected in groups depending on their final destination. Those that were traveling to Chicago, Cleveland,

Boston or other larger cities and vicinities in the Eastern United States were sent to the appropriate collection centers in the harbor.

In the collection centers the people were met by welfare organization representatives, who in most cases spoke the newcomers' native languages. These representatives provided the immigrants with tickets, mostly by train, told them who would meet them at their final destination and took them by bus to one of the two railroad stations in New York City: Pennsylvania and Grand Central stations. After an explanation of how to behave on the train, they were put on the train and sent to their final destination. Those that needed to travel for four hours or more received money to buy food on the train. Later I heard that for many people the little bit of food money was their first savings in America. Those that traveled to Los Angeles, San Francisco or other Western United States locations, were sent either by plane or train. Train travel took about three days.

There were small groups of lucky immigrants, including me, that did not need to worry how to get to their final destination. We were sent to another section of the harbor where our relatives awaited us. In addition, there were some well-known Lithuanian personalities, such as writers Antanas Gustaitis, Bernardas Brazdžionis, opera star Juzė

Augaitytė—whom I later got to know personally—and several military officers. They were all
met by the New York archdiocese and appropriate
Lithuanian parish representatives.

I was overjoyed when I found out, during my
document verification, that my relatives where
there to meet me. Oh what a meeting that was!
My Uncle Kukanskis, my Aunt Monica and Uncle
Raskauskas and my Cousin Leon Raskauskas, all
hugged each other, cried and hurried to my cousin's car. Waterbury, Connecticut is about 90 miles
from New York, but because the roads were good,
the travel time took about two hours including a
stop for a meal. I was terrified at the traffic and
swore silently, that if I survived that ride, I would
never travel in a car in such traffic. Of course, I
was comparing automobile traffic in Germany,
which was virtually nonexistent, with New York's
West Side Highway.

Another wonderful joy awaited me when we
arrived at my uncle's house. In the back yard there
were more than ten people—relatives who had
waited several hours for our arrival. The only person from the crowd I recognized was my Cousin
Peter Kukanskis, the one that came to Lithuania
in 1937. Some of the relatives I recognized from
pictures that my mother had. My Cousin Peter introduced me to other relatives and the feast began.

I would love to remember all the wonderful foods that were on the table, but all was mixed with the emotions, first impressions, and multiple questions and answers. I remember only that it was dark before the relatives departed and one must remember that in August the darkness comes late.

When we finally were left alone, my Aunt Monica took me to one of the bedrooms with two single beds. She explained that one of the beds was for me and the other was for my Cousin Leon. She also showed me a dresser with one drawer full of underwear and several shirts. She also informed me that the next day we would go to a clothing store and get some up-to-date clothes. The next day, after buying suits, sport jackets, pants and shaving necessities, my uncle took me to a barber shop where I got an American-style haircut, which was considerably shorter and simpler than my European haircut. I surmised that they were determined to make me look like an American rather than a poor European refugee. Of course, I did not resist these arrangements.

Later, when I had a chance to talk to other, newly arrived Lithuanian immigrants, I found out that their beginning was not as easy as mine, especially those that did not have relatives here. Families needed apartments, which were few with affordable prices. Many had to be content with one or two bedroom apartments, sometime even at the basement level. But compared to the refugee camp accommodations, where a family of six had to fit into one room, this type of apartment was a luxury. When I think back about my beginnings in the United States, I am forever grateful to my relatives who so generously accepted me and provided the easy beginnings.

## Making Ends Meet

The most important worry for the new immigrants was work. During the years 1949–1951 the United States unemployment rate was about 9%, therefore it was difficult to get any work. Getting work was especially difficult for professionals such as lawyers, teachers, former military officers, journalists and other professions that did not meet American standards. It was extremely difficult for those that could not speak English. For the professional the difficulty was not only the physical aspect of work but also the mental attitude. From the moral point of view imagine a lawyer, teacher or professional military officer enduring digging ditches or doing other hard physical work. In Europe these people did not have to do physical work; that was for the "masses," not for educated professionals.

On weekends they tried to gain some self-esteem, where in various gatherings, they addressed each other by their former titles and enumerated their former accomplishments, sometimes even embellishing them. Of course, there were exceptions. I met and became friends with the Stiklorius family. He was a judge in Lithuania, having been educated in law in Berlin, Germany; spoke fluent English, German, Polish and Russian in addition to his native Lithuanian, while his wife Taisa also had a good education and came from the Russian nobility.

They both were humble, had a great sense of humor and commendable attitude about life. It was always a pleasure to be in their company. He never wanted to accept his former status and if someone addressed him as "Your honor," with a smile he would comment: "I regret that today I am not sitting on the bench, therefore I cannot impose a fine for insulting my character". He worked at an insurance company's legal department until his retirement, but could never get admittance to the bar as there was always some flimsy excuse whenever he applied.

The other person with extraordinary humility was General Raštikis, who during Lithuanian independence was the chief of the Lithuanian Armed Forces. During his first year in the United States he worked as laborer in a machine shop. Some

Los Angeles newspaper reporter unmasked who he was and wrote a very flattering article. His boss was very embarrassed and gave him a better job. Later, Professor Klimas, who was working at Syracuse University, found Raštikis a job there as an instructor in the Russian language.

For the immigrants, the welfare organizations paid the first month's rent and gave money for a month's worth of food. It was considerably easier for those that had relatives; in emergencies they could help their immigrant relatives, even though many Lithuanians are independently minded and did not want to accept charity even from relatives.

Almost all Lithuanians, old and new, lived in one section of Waterbury, Connecticut, called Brooklyn. There was a Lithuanian church, bookstore, several stores and two Lithuanian clubs. All other nationalities, Italians, Germans, Poles, etc. also lived in their respective neighborhoods.

Many of the Lithuanian immigrants that settled in the vicinity of Waterbury found seasonal jobs at the tobacco farms—when the crops were harvested, the jobs ended. Another problem was that men working on the tobacco farms had to live in dormitories because the tobacco farms were about 30 miles away from Waterbury. Therefore, they could only see their families on weekends. In other words, many immigrants did not have an easy beginning in the United States.

My Uncle Kukanskis gave me a job at his plumbing shop. His jobs were mostly in the residential areas. Although the work was not to my liking, it was a job and I did not have to worry how I was going to make a living at that time. The second day after arrival I began to ask my uncle when I could start working. He answered that I could wait for a few weeks, because I was young and had many years of work ahead of me before retirement. My Aunt Monica also told me that she did not expect me to pay room and board for the next few weeks or longer.

As I was leisurely passing my first couple weeks, my Aunt Monica asked me to call Uncle Kukanskis to come for lunch. When he came home he was very surprised that I knew how to use a telephone. I explained to him that in Lithuania and Europe in general, the telephone was no longer a novelty, particularly in the cities. He only remembered that when he left Lithuania in 1905, there were hardly any telephones, hence he associated his knowledge with what he remembered.

After about two weeks in the United States, I was invited to attend a local Lithuanian picnic. That Sunday morning Uncle Kukanskis gave me $20 suggesting I buy some girl a drink and food. I was uncomfortable accepting the money and protested without success, with him further encouraging me to enjoy my first holiday in America. Finally, I accepted his gift and went to the picnic. Actually I had a very enjoyable time, made a few acquaintances, had a few beers and for the first time tasted American hot dogs.

## *Culture Shock*

Although my material beginnings in America were a good deal easier compared to other Lithuanians, the cultural shock was quite a different matter. What struck me most were young girls dressed in jeans and men's shirts, with the shirt tails sticking out and smoking cigarettes in public. At that time, that kind of behavior in Europe was totally unacceptable. I decided then that I would not marry any American girls that had that kind of behavior.

In the movie theaters, people entered and left the theater whenever they pleased, and while in the theater, had to have something to chew on or smoke which disturbed the other visitors. In Germany one could only enter or leave the theater before or after the movie. Smoking and eating in the theater was prohibited.

Another curiosity was the interaction between people after introductions, where people immediately started to call each other by their first names, not using prefixes such as mister, miss or a title.

Being used to a strict discipline of ethics in introductions, the use of first names among strangers was strange to me to say the least. Years later, I still had difficulty addressing my superiors by their first name. That inhibition is gone now along with my attitude toward young ladies who smoke in public.

Food preparation and service in the United States was also different from restaurants in Germany. One day my Cousin Leon suggested I take my girlfriend to dinner. Since I did not have a car my cousin let me drive his car. I already had learned how to drive in Germany, and by October 1949 I had my driver's license. I took my cousin's suggestion and one Sunday I and my girlfriend went to an excellent restaurant—at least by my standards back in those days—and ordered our meals. In Germany and in other European countries at that time, when one ordered a meal everything came together, that is: the salad, the soup, the main course and the dessert. The reason for this behavior was the fact that food in those days in most European countries was rationed and one had to use ration card coupons depending what was ordered.

Unbeknown to me, in the United States, all course meals came one at the time, hence first arrived the salad. We waited for a while until finally the waiter came and said something to us. Because my English was not that good, I did not understand him. I smiled and nodded my head. He took the salad away and brought the soup. Same routine; we waited a while, the waiter came, said something, I smiled and nodded my head. He took the soup away and brought the main course. By this time I said to my girlfriend, "Let's eat this serving before the waiter takes it away".

When I came home I told my cousin what had happened in the restaurant. He had a good laugh and explained how the food is served in the United States as well as in South American restaurants—he was born in Argentina. After that episode I was smarter than other Lithuanian immigrants and was able to explain to them how the food is served in United States restaurants, without telling them what it cost me to learn that lesson.

To be truthful, at that time American culture was so foreign to me that if I had the money I would have gone back to Germany. After several months, by the time I had the money, I had gotten used to American culture and had no desire to return to Germany. After some discussions with other recently-arrived Lithuanian refugees, I was glad to hear that their thinking was similar to mine.

## The First Jobs

After a couple of weeks of "vacations" I finally convinced Uncle Kukanskis that it was time for me to start working. He agreed and took me along to his plumbing shop. On the way we stopped at the gas station, where my uncle introduced me to the workers there. They asked me many questions, and I, with the help of my uncle, answered those questions. You may wonder why I needed my uncle's help…simple: I did not speak good enough English to carry on a conversation.

The questions at the gas station centered on life in Lithuania and Germany. It was interesting to note the wrong impressions that Americans had as to what was going on in post-war Germany. I could not understand their thinking; after all, many of the families had members who served in the United States Armed Forces and some of those had occupation duties in Germany. Later, when I had a chance to talk to my Cousins Leon and Peter, who both served in the Pacific and later in the occupation of Japan, as well as with some former service men who were in Germany, I began to understand better about the lack of accurate information regarding life in Germany. Most of the occupation duties required no contact with the local population, all supplies were brought in from the United States and the soldiers were discouraged from fraternization with the local population.

At work I had to quickly learn the American system of measurements. I was schooled in the metric system, while Americans were using inches, feet, yards, miles, gallons, ounces and pounds. Initially everything looked "Greek" to me. I could not tell the difference between a foot and an inch, much less to be able to tell how much of that was in the metric system. But I learned quickly because it was necessary for me to function intelligently at my work. I would take various fittings in sizes, write down the size and display those items in front of me and memorize, in my mind comparing them to the metric system. There was an additional value for me, because I learned the American system and instant translation to the metric system. Later in my career that knowledge was quite valuable.

A few decades ago the Congress wanted to change measurements to the metric system, but the results are meager. Near the Canadian and Mexican borders the distances are written in both kilometers and miles because both Canada and Mexico use the metric system. Product labels, in most cases, are written in metric and accepted American systems. Another interesting fact is that automobile and pharmaceutical concerns use the metric system.

I worked for about four months at my uncle's shop. As the winter approached the plumbing work decreased. I knew that my uncle would not let me go but I did not want to be a burden to his shop. I began to look for a new job. I explained to him what I had in mind and he agreed with me. He even complimented me that I had such good understanding about the economy. After a little while I found a job in the cinder block plant. Although it was hard work and long hours—12 hour days with six days per week—I was making about $100 a week, which at that time was very good money.

Although I was working long hours, I slowly began to study television technology—I already knew radio communications technology. At the same time I began to speak acceptable English, learning by reading newspapers and books. I made a point to learn at least 10 English words per day. All of this was necessary, because at work there were only three Lithuanian speakers among 60 workers. The long hours continued for about two years with no more than four hours of sleep a night. When I finally learned enough about television technology I bought a set of parts and assembled a TV, which to my surprise, worked.

I looked for and easily found work in a Radio and TV repair shop, repairing TVs, radios and installing TV antennas. Although the pay was somewhat less than in the cinder block plant, I needed to work only eight hours per day for six days a week. I knew that ultimately I wanted to work as an engineer, but I also understood that technology had advanced considerably since my days in school. To catch up to the technology of the day, I decided to take some math and physics refresher courses in a local university. I continued studies evenings and weekends. After about two-and-a-half years, the end of 1954, I felt that I had a solid understanding of the engineering sciences and decided to look for a job as an engineer.

In March 1955 I received American citizenship. During the ceremonies that were conducted in the court house and prior to taking the oath, the judge asked me if I wanted to Americanize my name. He explained that my name would be very difficult for Americans to pronounce. I answered him as follows: "Your honor, if I reach a high rank in my endeavors, people will learn how to pronounce my name. However, if I remain a simple laborer, it will not matter how my name is pronounced. My name was good for my father, my grandfather and my earlier ancestors; therefore it shall be good enough for me". So I left my name the same as it was when I was born. Later in life I learned that those that needed to learn how to pronounce my name did so, and for those that didn't, it did not matter.

# My Family

Although I was very busy at work and furthering my technical studies, I still found time to date a few girls. Those were pleasant dates at Saturday night dances, walks in the park, sometimes a movie and an occasional meal at a local restaurant. And by the way, all my dates were with newly arrived Lithuanian immigrant girls, for I had already decided that I would not date jeans-wearing, cigarette-smoking, American girls—I wish I had not made that decision at that time. This lasted for about a year after my arrival in the United States. In July of 1950 I began to date my future wife.

At first we did not talk about or consider getting married, but after seeing some of our friends become serious couples, we also began to talk about a wedding. My Aunt Monica and my future wife's mother tried to talk us out of getting married, for we both were young and I was working a lot and studying and would have very little time for my wife and potential children. But being young and in love, we dismissed suggestions from the more experienced and older people.

When I look back from today's perspective at what I experienced during my first marriage, it would have been better had I listened to the advice of people with more experience in married life. But as the American proverb says: "Don't cry over spilled milk". Although later in life I experienced many sorrows and mental pain, I do not regret the past for everything turned out just fine.

In the fall of 1950 we decided to get married at the end of December and I teasingly remarked that the wedding date would be easy to remember. Our wedding took place on December 30. My Aunt Monica did a lot of work for our wedding. She not only purchased all the food but also organized her lady friends to help her in the kitchen. My future in-laws were poor and contributed virtually nothing to the wedding expenses. My future mother-in-law had arrived in the United States with two children about a year-and-a-half

before our wedding and my future father-in-law
came only six months before the wedding.

The wedding was performed in the Lithuanian Roman Catholic Church and the reception
was held in the Lithuanian club. We received a lot
of presents from our friends and relatives. An especially large gift of $200 came from my Uncle
Kukanskis. At that time it was a lot of money. The
five-day honeymoon was spent in New York—we
even greeted the New Year in Times Square.

## *Precious Children and the Death of a Marriage*

Arriving home after the honeymoon there
was work, studies, finding an apartment, purchasing furniture and other implements needed for a
new family. Although my income was just average
we were happy. My wife found work and by putting our earnings together we could live reasonably comfortably even by American standards, and
quite well compared to newly arrived Lithuanian
immigrants.

My wife became pregnant a month after our
wedding and soon had to quit work. Fortunately,
in the meantime, I got a raise and we could continue to live better than most of the new immigrants.

In June of 1951 North Korea attacked South
Korea. Because the United States had their troops
stationed there and had signed a mutual defense

assistance agreement, it became involved in the conflict. The politicians called it a police action and according to the American constitution, the president did not need congressional approval or a declaration of war to send American armed forces into harm's way. The name of that conflict did not matter, in the end it required over 50,000 American lives, more than 150,000 wounded or missing in action and it took over three years. At that time fear of the communists, primarily the sponsor of the conflict—the Soviet Union, led the newly elected president, General Eisenhower, the winner of the European war, to consider using nuclear weapons to defeat North Korea.

The hatred of communism and the desire to contribute to its destruction enticed many young Lithuanian men, including me, to volunteer for the American Armed Forces. At the beginning of the conflict the American Selective Service did not take non-American citizens. As time passed, and as the casualties in Korea mounted, non-citizens began to be accepted, primarily in the army. I registered with the Selective Service as a volunteer, but was not accepted because I was married. After about six months even married men were being accepted.

In the acceptance application there was a question asking if you had children. I answered that my wife was pregnant. On the basis of that information, I was not accepted for service in the United States Armed Forces although my desire was to make a career in the United States military.

Linda was born October 15, 1951. It was a joyous occasion not only for us but also for our relatives. She was a beautiful baby, did not cry; it was a sheer joy to have her and watch her grow. Time passed swiftly and interestingly, a year-and-a-half later, my wife was pregnant again. On July 22, 1953 a boy was born. We gave him two Lithuanian names: Aidas (Echo) and Leonas (Leon). Immediately after the birth he looked very weak. Three-and-a-half days later, after receiving the last rights and sacraments, as is customary in the Roman Catholic Church, he died. He was buried in Calvary Cemetery, Waterbury, Connecticut. The doctor said he died of congestive heart failure. In those days we knew little about infant sicknesses and trusted the doctor's word. Today, knowing more, I might be looking for a second opinion. Although it was very painful to lose a son, time has healed fatherly sorrow.

On April 11, 1957 our son Dante was born. It was a great joy. He was lively, engaging and by a few months old always smiled. When he was about three-and-a-half years old, my wife received a telephone call from Linda's school demanding that she come and pick up her son. Because the school was close to our house, Linda was walking to school and apparently Dante followed her. When I came home from work my wife told me the story. To me it was incomprehensible that she would not miss our son. I do not remember now what explanation she gave me. This was probably my first suspicion that she was not paying much attention to the welfare of our children.

On July 17, 1961 our daughter Carla was born. I was overjoyed and hoped that our married life, which was beginning to unravel at that time, would improve. However, that did not happen. Somehow we managed to live together for almost two more years but finally separated. As is the custom in the United States, the wife gets the custody of the children while the father must provide support. At that time it was not customary, and I was not smart enough, to claim that she was a drug addict and the children's custody should be awarded to me.

In reality, our married life began to fall apart around 1957, soon after Dante's birth. In front of our friends and relatives she became obnoxiously pretentious by demanding that she receive proper respect as an engineer's wife. I tried to tell her that there are good people irrespective of their positions in life. She even began to refuse making visits to her parents, because they were uneducated and had menial jobs. She loved to get dressed up and to show her beauty to her friends and complete strangers.

The overall difficulty that affected our marriage was that she began to use narcotics. In the fifth decade of the twentieth century that was a rarity. At the beginning I did not know what was happening; sometimes she would be quite sensible while at other times she acted as if she was insane. I was afraid what she might do to the children.

Sometimes, when I came back from work, I found that the children were not fed, dishes not washed and her hands shook when she held a cup of coffee. Later I found out that the coffee was laced with narcotics.

About six months before our separation I found out that she had a lover. I found that out from her lover's wife, who was asking that I try to separate them, for she wanted him back. At that point I was skeptical about our ability to live together as husband and wife. When I tried to tell her that I knew of her infidelity she created a scene. That was the last episode in our married life.

While living apart I visited the children and brought them gifts. I had hardly any conversations with the wife, although I behaved with civility. Knowing that she was a narcotic addict, I began to plan how to get custody of the children. The day after Christmas of 1963, I met her, the children and her lover in a hotel parking lot ready for a journey. She told me that she was going to Las Vegas where she hoped to get a quick divorce. I asked her to leave the children with me but she refused. She also was using my car and declined to give it back to me. I surmised that my car was the only transportation she and her lover had.

After a couple of months I received a telephone call from a children's home in Las Vegas stating that my children were placed there by their mother's boyfriend. I had a conversation with my daughter Linda, who at that time was 12 years old. She asked if I would bring them back to me. I assured her that I would do so as fast as I could, but no longer than a few days. I told her to take good care of her brother and sister and not to worry. The manager of the children's home agreed to take them to the airport as soon as I sent her tickets. The next day the tickets arrived and that evening I met them in New York's airport with love and joy.

I raised my children alone for about two years. I found a responsible woman who babysat during the day, fed them and took care of them and sometimes, when I had to go out of town overnight or longer on business, stayed at the house with them.

Life with the children continued without much excitement. Linda and Dante were going to school while Carla was growing without missing her mother. Each summer I let them go and visit their grandparents. From the children I surmised that their grandparents suffered greatly over the disappearance of their daughter, although personally I avoided involving myself in such conversations with them. This chapter of my life's book was closed!

## *False Start, Fresh Start*

After a while I started dating a lady, who in the passage of time became my second wife. We got married in the summer of 1965. She had two boys and a daughter from her first marriage. She was sympathetic and tried to be a mother for my children. At the beginning of the marriage, life was going in the right direction. After melding our two families together, we established equilibrium and it appeared that a happy future was assured. The children got along well and we both tried and wanted to be successful in our life together.

Economically our life was improving; we bought a house, Linda was going to a private Lithuanian high school that was supervised by Lithuanian nuns in Putnam, Connecticut. The Lithuanian nuns had a good influence on her, retaining the heritage, language and customs of Lithuania. To this day, Linda can speak, read and write Lithuanian and remembers the customs of her ancestors. Dante went to a military prep school. My wife's two boys, being about the same age as Dante also went to military prep schools.

At home, left with her daughter and Carla, we began to travel whenever I needed to go somewhere on business. On the surface everything appeared to be fine but somehow things began to fall apart. First it was the comparisons she made between her children and mine. In my opinion I felt that comparisons were unjustified and occasionally I told her so. For example: Linda was an exceptionally good student while her daughter was just average. Dante's school work was better than her younger son's, but the problem was that Dante managed to get into trouble and required some disciplinary action. Her older son could not get along with us and went to live with his father. That was another cause of misunderstanding, although her older son was living with his father before we started dating and before our marriage.

After a while it looked like everything was settled. Her daughter got married and had a daughter, a granddaughter for my wife and me. However, the deep seated animosity toward my children became evident. She began to almost hate Carla, accusing her of all sorts of misdeeds like stealing her lipstick and scarves. This was not true because after a while she found her lipstick and scarves. And, at that time Carla did not use lipstick at home or in school.

I never thought that married life could fall apart so quickly and, what appeared to be, without a good cause and justification. In December 1977, we separated. Because the other children were no longer living with us, Carla and I found an apartment and moved out of the house. Carla was still in high school and helped me with housework.

For the following two months or so I did not go anywhere. I sank into a dark mood over the thoughts of what had happened to my life—questions that did not have satisfactory answers. I continued in my work, but more like a robot without feelings or joy. Carla, seeing my depression, urged me to go out, enjoy life and find a woman who could cheer me up. When I told her I did not know a woman who would cheer me up, she suggested that I should invite Fran, who was the secretary in our office, for dinner and a dance. (Carla knew Fran from the times she came to my office to nag and beg me to use my car, if only for a few hours, because she already had her driver's license).

Finally I listened to Carla and asked Fran out on a date. She informed me that she was planning to go out that evening with her girlfriend. I was not sure if she wanted to get rid of me or if she was really going out with another girl. Well, I invited them both to dinner and dance and wondered what the outcome would be. I felt that in time I could get rid of her girlfriend and that other evenings would be ours. Although I had an eye on Fran I did not expect that anyone else would notice it. Evidently, after that evening her girlfriend told Fran that I was paying attention to Fran and not her; so started my friendship with Fran without interference from her girlfriend.

At first it appeared that we were passing our time together merely to forget our loneliness. After all, she was about fourteen years younger than I, and besides, as I remembered she had a boyfriend. With the passage of time the attraction and affection for each other grew. We enjoyed each other's company and, at least I was delighted to be with her—but I was not sure about her feelings.

Here I have to relate one interesting incident. Fran was a good cook and asked me if I knew any Lithuanian dishes. I told her that I knew how to make Lithuanian "cepelinai" (meatball encased in potato dough) and told her, that given the first opportunity, I would be delighted to make this delicious Lithuanian dish at her apartment. After bringing all the necessary ingredients for "cepelinai," she cheerfully asked what she could do to help me. I cheerfully told her that she could peal 20 pounds of potatoes. She informed me that she had to clean the apartment and left me alone to do the cooking. Cepelinai was a success because Fran and her children liked it. Even to this day I occasionally prepare this delicious Lithuanian dish, although Fran does not participate in the preparation.

Our love and devotion to each other grew slowly. At that time I was very careful about involving myself emotionally with women because as an American proverb says: "Burned twice, careful trice". Our children did not have anything against our friendship or spending our free time together; in reality they wanted not just friendship but marriage. Fran's two children, Stephen and David, liked me, and Carla was satisfied that I finally found a woman who was able to make me happy.

One day David, who at that time was about nine years old, asked me if he could call me daddy. I told him that I would be delighted if he called me daddy. Fran and I were careful although we trusted each other. We began to travel together, spend vacations together and I managed to burden her with the payment of my bills, because I am very negligent in that department. Six years had passed in our loving relationship and we finally decided to get married. Our wedding took place on March 10, 1984, which was exactly six years from our first date.

After our children were educated and started their own families, Fran and I were left to blissfully spend our time, well most of the time, reminiscing on the past and with anticipation looking forward to the future.

One particular item that I want to mention is my mother's question when she saw us in 1989. She wanted to know if our marriage was performed in a church. I explained to her that Fran is not a Roman Catholic, therefore our wedding took place in another Christian denomination; let her rest in peace knowing the truth.

# Chapter V

## My Career and Professional Work

Having US citizenship, an engineering degree and being able to speak reasonably good English, I began to think about finding work in my specialty. The opportunity came rather quickly. One day I noticed in the local newspaper an advertisement by IBM looking for engineers. I sent my resume to the designated address and in a couple of weeks received an invitation for an interview locally in Waterbury, Connecticut.

After the first interview I received an invitation to visit the IBM offices in Poughkeepsie, New York. The second interview took all day. I met several engineers who questioned me not only on technical matters but family attitudes, for example: would my wife be willing to move, do we have children, etc. At that point I silently praised myself for having the foresight to take the engineering refresher courses earlier, because some of the technical questions were exactly what I had learned. My last discussion was with one of the personnel managers. I do not remember all the details related to IBM personnel and employment policies, I only remember that he told that in a couple of weeks I would hear from IBM in writing.

So began the nerve-wrecking wait. Two of my neighbors asked me what I had done, because they were questioned by the FBI about my character. (In those days it was legal for companies to have police or the FBI investigate a potential employee's personal information.) Finally a letter from IBM arrived offering me a position as a junior engineer in the product testing department. Later I found out that that department had about 100 engineers and technicians. The start date was June 1, 1955. I was delighted that I finally could work in my profession and in a highly respected company.

We invited friends for a party to celebrate my future as an engineer. One must appreciate that there were very few new immigrants that were able to get jobs as engineers, which considered a very prestigious job amongst Lithuanian immigrants. Never mind that the salary was only half compared to what I was earning as a TV repairman; my starting salary at IBM was $75 a week, while as a TV repairman I earned $150 a week.

In two weeks we had to find an apartment, moving company, pack everything and move from Waterbury, Connecticut to Poughkeepsie, New York. IBM agreed to pay for my moving expenses and gave us two weeks' worth of living expenses.

## *Work at IBM*

The first three weeks at IBM were spent in orientation. After receiving written and verbal information about the company, we were led to various departments where we heard what each department was doing and how we would be able to work together to make a better IBM. We also were taken to the IBM Country Club and explained about the reduced costs for food, beverages, ice cream and various sports activities for workers and their families.

There was one item that was explained very specifically: alcohol. We were told that alcohol was prohibited from being "on the person" or "inside the person". Anyone caught with alcohol during working hours would be dismissed immediately. If an IBM employee was caught drunk by authorities outside the work hours, he or she would receive a reprimand while a second offense meant dismissal. These policies were promulgated by the company's president Thomas Watson. Later, his son, Thomas Watson, Jr. maintained his father's policies regarding work and, to some extent, the private lives of IBM employees.

Not far from their laboratories IBM had a guest house which, by any standard, was comparable to a high-class hotel. Visiting dignitaries and potential customers were housed and fed, for the hotel had a very good restaurant. But alcoholic beverages were not permitted.

IBM had excellent employee benefits and allowed liberal policies in family emergencies. For example: if a member of the family was sick, the worker was sent home with pay to take care of the family member. At that time IBM was the only company to have such liberal benefits. Although salaries were perhaps somewhat lower compared to other companies, the benefits and the care of employees and their families outweighed the lower salaries. Consequently, IBM had very dedicated and loyal employees.

All engineers, technicians and managers were required to wear dark blue suits, white shirts and conservative striped ties. In the laboratories we were required to wear lab overcoats that were furnished by IBM.

## My Career and Professional Work

After three weeks of orientation and wandering through various departments I finally found out where, in that big organization, I would be working. To my delight I was assigned to work in the computer testing department. Internally we called ourselves computer specialists while to people outside we referred to ourselves as working with "electronic brains".

After barely getting familiar with my assigned work I was sent for a month to another IBM location in Endicott, New York to learn the operations and technical details for IBM's calculating/printing machine, because there was no one in my department that knew anything about this device. IBM paid for me and the family's travel and living expenses—another demonstration on how IBM took care of their families.

After a month I came back to my department and began my assigned work. The work was very interesting, everything new, unknown and there was no book to refer to or find what was unknown. When we made testing or discoveries, we had to keep very detailed logs and, at the end of the project, write a technical report. Those reports or their parts were collected, printed and used as technical books throughout IBM. This was the birth of computer technical journals and books that were distributed through the universities and laboratories of the world.

After almost two years I was promoted to the senior engineer's position, IBM's name for this position was "Associate Engineer," with larger responsibilities and more money. In this new position several engineers and technicians worked for me and I had responsibility for larger projects. This position was also in the ranks of first line management and we were paid once every two weeks instead of the normal once a week.

My new responsibility required me to travel on business to various US cities. Not only work but the experience of travel was very interesting. I had an opportunity to learn more about American cities and culture. Travel revealed to me that the United States is not a monolithic country; immigrants from many different countries, congregating in various cities of the United States created a unique American culture.

The difference between different cities was enormous. For example: New Orleans, Louisiana was quite different from Baltimore, Maryland which was very different from New York City. Various religions, customs and foods that were brought from their native countries enriched American attitudes and tolerance for all living here. In those days there were exceptions, especially for blacks, American Indians and certain religious practices. In some parts of the country they were treated as second class citizens and sometimes were persecuted unjustly. Over the decades things have changed and today we have much more equal treatment of all citizens and non-citizen residents.

The year 1957 was rewarding for me not only at work but also in my family. First, our son Dante was born on April 11. Another important event was the permission from the Soviet authorities to send packages to relatives in Lithuania and other Soviet republics. There were packaging and forwarding organizations, specially licensed by the Soviet Union that inspected the goods and prepared a content manifest. At the same time they collected duties, which usually were the same as the price of the goods being sent. We knew that this money was being used for the subversive activities of Soviet spies in the United States.

Although it was very painful knowing the purpose of the collected dollars, the desire to help our Lithuanian relatives, even in a small way, outweighed this nefarious undertaking by the Bolsheviks. Those small packages, even with the severe restrictions of what and how much could be sent, gave us at least some consolation knowing that the goods would, in a small way, enlighten and enrich their drab, joyless daily lives.

## *Promotions*

IBM had developed an excellent methodology to further professional careers. Junior and senior engineers in the laboratories performed technical work. The next promotion divided engineers in two groups: those that were slated for a technical future were promoted in the staff engineering ranks while those that were deemed to be future managers were promoted to project engineering positions. At that time I thought that those separations paid no attention to specific past schooling and experience.

IBM also had very well-prepared high-level technical and general educational evening courses for employees. We could take any courses but in our laboratories, engineers took mostly technical subjects associated with the work while the managers studied humanitarian and marketing courses. Attendance at the courses, books and other supplies were free and the courses were taught by qualified IBM employees and professors from local universities.

The evening courses were voluntary while the courses directly related to work were conducted during the day. The candidates for such courses had to be recommended by their department manager. In 1958 IBM decided that all new product research and development would be conducted with transistors rather than vacuum tubes. The problem was that IBM had only a handful of transistor experts. A massive educational program was instituted. My manager recommended me for these full-time courses which lasted 16 weeks. For me it was not only an honor but also an opportunity to broaden my technical knowledge.

When we came back after 16 weeks of schooling the manager told me that I would be transferred to a new department to develop a new transistor-based product. I explained to him that I had only the transistor theory and not transistor application's knowledge. He said: "OK, you will have to go for 16 more weeks to learn transistor applications". So I started another 16 weeks of my additional technical education.

After finishing those courses, I was transferred to a development department working on a new transistorized machine. I was also promoted to project engineer, which meant that IBM saw me as a potential manager, not a technical scientist. I was not very satisfied with this promotion because I wanted to be a scientist, but kept my mouth shut. Looking back from the current perspective, it seems IBM knew better than me about my future potential.

When I was promoted to the project engineer position and had responsibility for eight engineers and five or six technicians, I often wondered how I would feel if, living in Lithuania, my boss would be a foreigner. I probably would have been jealous and or resented that a foreigner was giving me orders. Fortunately, at IBM I did not experience such an attitude and slowly learned how to live with my situation and be thankful for it.

Life was going well and from a professional standpoint I could not complain. On the home front, we had some savings and decided to buy a house. We were a real typical American family, two children, good job, new car, a new house, in other words, just live and enjoy. However, in my personal life dark clouds began to gather. I thought maybe I was working too much and did not pay enough attention to the family. I reduced my evening courses and eventually stopped them altogether because my wife thought that I was educated enough.

In early 1961, my boss left IBM to work in an IBM competitor organization: UNIVAC. About two months after he left IBM, I received a telephone call from him inquiring if I would be interested in discussing opportunities at UNIVAC. My wife was tired of living in the IBM "family" and was looking for new adventures, therefore she welcomed this invitation.

A week later I visited my former boss and discussed the possibility of working in his new company. After a walk through the factory and laboratories I came to the conclusion that UNIVAC would offer many challenges. From the technical standpoint, UNIVAC products were superior to IBM, but from the standpoint of sales, marketing and promotion as well as PR, was way behind IBM. I understood that accepting this new position I would have to sacrifice my time and devote myself more to the new job than what I had at IBM. After discussing the situation with my wife, she agreed to move to the new location, even if it was about three times more distant from her parents—a fact that was not really important to her.

Everything was settled; I received a substantial increase in salary, a promotion and agreed to start work on June 1, 1961, exactly six years to the day from my starting date in IBM.

### *Work and Travels at UNIVAC*

My first day in the new job was a big shock. Although during the interview I observed many shortcomings in UNIVAC compared to IBM, I never expected such a huge mess. Nobody seemed to know what was going on or knew what to do if something did not work. After such "greetings" I went to my former and current boss asking for advice. His answer was very simple: "Working at IBM you displayed ingenuity not only how to solve problems but also the ability to circumvent irrelevant directives and I am sure you will find ways to do so here".

After receiving such instructions I began to act. In the first place, I discharged about one-fourth of the old mangers, who thought that they were guaranteed pensions without much effort. The ones that were left began to ask if the same fate awaited them. To those inquiries I answered simply: "Carry out your duties honestly and to the best of your ability and do not worry about the future. However, if you do not know how to do your present job, let me know and I will try to find you something according to your abilities". Needless to say, my boss received numerous complaints but he did not interfere and defended my position. After several months some semblance of discipline and order was in place. Assigned tasks were carried out with satisfactory results.

As I have mentioned earlier, from the technical standpoint, UNIVAC products were superior to IBM, but the quality of products and sales methods were substantially inferior to IBM. Because IBM had a leading position, anyone that could not communicate with IBM equipment had no opportunity to sell in the IBM dominated market. At that time, the most prevalent communications media was magnetic tape. UNIVAC had a unique operating system, different from IBM magnetic tape code.

In 1960, before I started work at UNIVAC, the company decided to develop an IBM compatible magnetic tape drive. Because I had experience in IBM tape drives, I was asked to develop such a product. In six or seven months my engineering group was able to design a reliable IBM compatible tape drive.

This achievement brought me a promotion to a product line manager position with more responsibility and a higher salary. From the professional standpoint, this was my most enjoyable period in the service of UNIVAC. Various business travels, not only in United States as well as Europe, gave me an opportunity to learn about other countries cultures and customs.

Over a number of years I had the pleasure to visit Italy, their capital Rome, Saint Peter's Basilica, the Fountain of Trevi, the Coliseum and many other Italian architectural wonders in Florence, Venice and Milan. I had an opportunity to visit Paris and its notable monuments, such as Napoleon's tomb, Notre Dame Cathedral, the Louvre Museum, the Eiffel Tower and many other interesting spots in Paris. I cannot forget to mention the beautiful principality of Monte Carlo and the well-known gambling casino (Monte Casino), where on occasion I "managed" to lose small sums of money—when compared to real gamblers.

Switzerland left me unforgettable impressions of their cleanliness, orderliness and mountainous beauty and the fact that in the midst of tumultuous Europe they had not had a war for over three hundred years. I had an opportunity to ski in the beautiful Swiss Alps in Zumwalt and Gstaat. Austria equals Switzerland in the beauty of her Alps. I was left with an unforgettable impression about the capital, Vienna. Vienna, even to this day, maintains the decorum of aristocratic beauty, having been the capital of the Austro-Hungarian Empire. I had an opportunity to visit the indescribable beauty and opulence of the imperial palace, the opera house and St. Stephen's Cathedral. I stayed in the well-known Sacher Hotel and ate at the restaurant that created the Sacher torte (cake) for the Emperor Franz-Josef II, which even to this day is available in the hotel restaurant and is being shipped on order to all parts of the world.

I hardly recognized Germany, which I left in 1949. It had developed an enviable economy and rebuilt many of the war-destroyed cities. This was the mark of German industriousness, work ethic and the Teutonic discipline.

Writing about middle Europe, I cannot forget Belgium and Holland. Belgium left me an impression—small in size, at one time a colonial empire, using two official languages and two (French and Dutch) cultures, managed to develop an industrial powerhouse and an international political base. The buildings in Brussels, especially the Royal Palace, rival in beauty with other notable buildings in Europe.

Holland, known for its windmills, is an exceptionally clean and orderly country. Those windmills, at one time used as water pumps, now are converted to restaurants or left as museum pieces. The current water control is all electrified. In the Middle Ages the Dutch were merchants and developed an excellent merchant marine. Before the Second World War she was a colonial empire, but today Holland is smaller in size than Lithuania, but has over nine million people. During the war their cities, especially Rotterdam, were destroyed by the Germans and Allies, but industrious Dutch managed to rebuild the cities and develop industries. It is important to remember that about one-third of Holland is below sea level. The most impressive creations are the dikes that prevent the flooding of the flat land, which is what Holland is all about. On top of the dikes there are super highways ringing most of Holland. The international airport of Schipol is about 30 feet below sea level. Today Holland has medieval buildings that harmonize well with the modern architecture. One cannot forget the Dutch canals that serve a very useful purpose. The canals are water runoff "roads" because Holland is so flat without any noticeable elevation.

In general, understanding different cultures broadened my outlook on the world and I became more of an international person. I am having a difficult time imagining that this village boy had the opportunity to see and visit the dreamed of places of Europe, the United States and other world countries, about which I will write later.

After four years working at the UNIVAC location in New York State, I was offered a position in UNIVAC headquarters in the Philadelphia suburbs as director of advanced development. It was a promotion and an increase in salary. In the fall of 1965 we moved to Pennsylvania.

The work was very interesting and required dedication on my part. My immediate supervisor was Press Eckert, the inventor of the computer. He possessed extraordinary intelligence and peculiarities; one could consider him bordering on genius. Sometimes, at the end of the day, without finishing a technical conversation, we would go home. Then maybe ten or eleven o'clock in the evening he would call me and continue the conversation that we had five hours prior, without any preliminaries. He could not understand why I needed to think for a minute about what we were talking about in the laboratory. Later, reading about Einstein's behavior I understood Press Eckert.

The year 1968 was the incubation of new technological companies that grew like mushrooms after a rain storm. I received an offer to start a new company with a former coworker. I told him that I did not have the kind of money necessary for a start-up company. He said that he was in contact with some people with money who were interested in my participation in starting a new technical product development and production company. After several months and many conversations and meetings, I agreed to participate and be the leader in the new, high risk, company. I reluctantly submitted my resignation to UNIVAC because I liked the work and my superior.

## *Digital Information Devices*

In June of 1968 I founded a new company, Digital Information Devices. Various documents associated with the new company's formation, such as the name registration and permits, required the legal profession's involvement. This was my first contact with various governmental agencies. After a few weeks, we had a company and the required permits, allowing us to conduct business in computer equipment.

The new laboratory had about 12 coworkers, mostly engineers. Because I had a lot of contacts with professionals I had no problem in recruiting highly qualified engineers. I already had the preliminary functional specifications of the machine therefore the engineers could immediately start the development work. The machine was for the "direct entry of data from keyboard to magnetic tape," abbreviated "Key-to-Tape". Up to that point data entry was done using IBM or UNIVAC cards which were punched on a special machine. Those cards were then entered directly into a computer or transcribed to a magnetic tape. In December of that year we demonstrated our new machine at a computer show in San Francisco. It was a record short production time for development of such a complicated device. My former associates were astonished at the results.

I participated with the development but not as much as I would have liked, because my duties as president of the company required me to attend to other non-technological matters. There were issues in which I had no experience and I had to learn fast if the company was to prosper. The chairman of the board, owner of a plastics factory, who invested a substantial amount of money in our company, assisted me and taught me a great deal. I was grateful to him for the business lessons

I received.

In March of 1969 we became a public company with stock traded on the Over the Counter (OTC) exchange. (Currently this market is called NASDAQ.) Here I again had to learn fast about the laws governing securities of publicly traded companies. And there were many of them, starting with the Securities and Exchange Commission created in 1934 with many modifications in later years. These laws were promulgated to protect investors from the outrageous abuses that occurred before 1934. Some of the leaders of these early companies were caught in rather nefarious undertakings to fatten their own pockets at the expense of the investors. Most of them were punished, but many escaped with the help of clever lawyers who found various loopholes in the laws. Hearing and reading about what has happened recently with the corporate shenanigans and virtual robbery by a few leaders of companies, one has to wonder if the guilty parties will go to jail or clever lawyers will get them off. In my opinion they should be hung in public; the 1930s revisited in 2002!

Our company started production in April of 1969. Because we already had sold a substantial number of machines, we needed larger production facilities. Plans for the building were made late in 1968 and construction started in early 1969.

The building was finished in July of 1969 and after moving in we started mass production.

The business was going along well. In 1972 we developed another machine, a small tape drive that could accept one-half inch tape which was the exchange media of all computers. Now we had two different products. The marketing of these products required different methods. I found a marketing vice president that, in my opinion, was very capable to do the job. However, my chairman of the board disagreed with me, even though he let me have it my way.

## *Overseas Expansion*

At the same time we decided to expand our business to Europe and Japan. This expansion required my personal attention. Expansion in Europe was not very difficult because I had acquaintances in Europe and was familiar with European business practices. Japan was an entirely different matter. In those days there were not many experts that knew the business methods of Japan. I met with a couple professors in Philadelphia who knew something about Japanese culture. I also found some books in the public library dealing with Japanese business behavior. After listening to the professors and reading the books, I finally traveled to Japan.

Japan, even to this day, is still very different in business matters and culture compared to the United States and European behavior—in the 1970s, Japan was a very different world. Very quickly I had to learn about daytime business matters and also socializing in the evening. The Japanese are very polite and hospitable. The politeness varies depending on the real or perceived status of the guest. In Japan handshakes are not accepted and when they meet there is a ritual of bowing to each other. The one that is of a lower rank bows deeper while the higher ranking individual bows less. This ritual is repeated several times. Before leaving for Japan I found out that for non-Japanese bowing is not required, a handshake is sufficient. Their customs revere age, white hair has preference in speaking, groups wait for the advice and wisdom from the elders, while the younger nod their heads in agreement. Contradicting an elder in a public gathering is unheard.

I remember one very interesting event. About eight Japanese and I were in a conference room standing while waiting for their superior to enter the room. Finally the superior came in and walked to the end of the table. Behind him there was a beautifully framed picture of an elder Japanese gentleman. The boss and all others turned towards the picture bowed a couple of times and then all set down. Later I found out the picture was of the founder of the company who lived in the nineteenth century.

Their food and eating habits are quite different compared to Western food and table manners. The food is cut into bite size pieces that can be consumed effectively using chop sticks, which is the accepted method in Japan. Nowadays we can readily find Japanese restaurants in the United States, but in the 1970s only a few Japanese restaurants could be found in Hawaii and a couple major cities on West Coast of the US.

While in Japan, I learned to eat raw fish, sushi. I misunderstood the language when my host asked if I liked "fresh fish". I, visualizing a skillet with a beautiful fish being fried, answered affirmatively. What he really meant was raw fish. Actually, after learning how to eat it I liked it and to this day occasionally I go to a sushi bar for a Japanese-style meal.

Beginning in 1970, until my retirement, I visited Japan ten or more times. Today Japanese life is quite different than it was 20-30 years ago. City streets in major cities are written in Japanese and English, there are European- and American-style restaurants that use forks and knives. Of course, even in Western-style restaurants one can find Japanese foods. In Tokyo there is a MacDonald's where one can get a real American hamburger or Japanese food.

My first trip to Japan was successful because I brought home a contract for a large number of our machines. We just had to design a Katakana character set and appropriate keyboard. That was not a difficult undertaking and after a few months we were shipping a Japanese version of the Key-to-Tape machine to Japan.

Everything was going reasonably well with my company. The only issue that surfaced was a difference of opinion with my chairman over future growth. Because he had a much larger stake in the company than me, and sensing that we would not be able to reconcile our differences, I suggested that he buy me out. He finally agreed. A couple months later I resigned and was paid for my share of the company. Regrettably, the company survived for about two years and was sold again for very little money, but it was no longer my concern.

# Chapter VI

## Lithuania, U.S. Politics and
## a New Start-up Company

In the spring of 1972, after selling my interest in Digital Information Devices and before starting something new, my wife and I decided to travel to Lithuania—a country that was still under the yoke of the Soviet Union. It was impossible for me to describe the feelings and heartache that that journey entailed. Before we left the United States, many of my friends and acquaintances tried to talk me out of the trip, because all, including myself, expected that I would be arrested and tried So-viet style by a kangaroo court as a "traitor of the fatherland". Even in the best of circumstances, I

97

thought I would be deported back to the United States, because I refused to go back to Communist-occupied Lithuania after the war and besides had been an officer of the German Air Force.

However, my desire to see my parents, relatives and the country of my birth after 28 years outweighed all the potential unpleasantness and potential danger from the Soviet authorities. My reasoning was that by the time the Soviet bureaucracy figured out who I was, I would have left their "paradise" and the gulags and been able to show them my "middle finger" from United States territory. I also had some potential protection from a few members of the United States Congress and from the American presidential candidate, Mr. Nixon, because I was a delegate to the Republican National Convention and Mr. Nixon was traveling to the Soviet Union at about the same time as my trip. I was advised to be in close contact via telephone with the US Embassy in Moscow wherever I traveled and when I arrived in Moscow to visit the Embassy.

It is impossible to describe what I felt that late evening when the plane landed in Vilnius. I do not have appropriate words and do not think that there are words in any language to properly describe my feelings. What a joy it was to see my aging parents and more than ten relatives. With tears running down my mother's tired face, I think that the hugging and kissing lasted more than ten minutes.

We were assigned rooms in the Hotel Neringa on Gediminas Street. As much as I remember, we and the relatives squeezed in a small room and celebrated until the early hours of the next morning. Before the celebration I got permission from the manager to purchase several bottles of Soviet-produced champagne and cognac after giving him a "small" gift of American cigarettes. I also asked the manager to allow my parents to stay with me but was told that the hotel was reserved for foreign visitors only.

In Vilnius we were permitted to stay only five days and were not allowed to leave the city limits. When asked why we could not stay longer in Vilnius, I was told that there were not enough hotel rooms for foreign visitors, although the floor on which we stayed had only three occupied rooms, including ours, during our stay.

I remember one peculiar Soviet rule. When I asked permission to leave the city limits and go visit my birthplace, it was explained to me that my rented car had no permit to travel outside the city limits. When I offered to rent a car that had a permit to travel outside the city I was told that on that day and for the next five days there was no driver available who could travel to that province. When I told them that I only had three days left in Vilnius, one of the officials with a smiling face regretted the situation and suggested that perhaps the next time when I visit Vilnius I should try to arrange travel outside the city in advance. (I am certain he knew exactly how many days I had left to stay in Vilnius.)

I cannot forget the meeting with my Cousin Valė Vegienė, for she and her family lived in Vilnius. She invited us all to her house for dinner. I knew she and her husband, Jonas, took a risk inviting foreigners to their house irrespective that these foreigners were her relatives. As long as I live, I will remember Valė and Jonas showing hospitality despite the obvious danger, and assign a special relationship with them.

The five days in Vilnius passed as a blink of an eye. We had to "move" to Riga, Latvia where we were permitted to stay up to fifteen days. I convinced my parents and my sister to come to Riga and spend a little more time with me. I succeeded in getting rooms for my parents and sister not only in the same hotel where I stayed but even on the same floor. Under Soviet rule visitors from foreign countries could not choose a hotel, it was assigned to them. I succeeded in getting the rooms after a meeting with the hotel manager and giving her the "small" gifts of French perfume, a carton of American cigarettes and agreeing to pay the bill in US dollars directly to her. Our guide, who was also our driver, took us beyond the 25 kilometer (approximately 15 miles) restricted limit all the way to Jarmala, a seaside resort town, after we gave him the gift of a carton of American cigarettes.

The 15 days in Riga with my parents passed as a short pleasant dream. While we were parting my mother said: "Son, I do not think we will ever see each other alive". She was right regarding seeing my father, who passed away in 1988. But I was able to visit mother numerous times after Lithuania became independent, starting in 1989 when my wife, Fran, and I paid her a visit in Plutiškės, where I grew up. She had an opportunity to meet her daughter-in-law and was delighted to learn that we were married in a church.

One day, before departing from Riga, I learned from a waitress with whom I established very good trust, how the KGB was "watching and making certain that nothing 'bad' happens to me". At that time she also told me that a young man in Kaunas set himself on fire, by pouring gasoline on himself, as a protest against the Soviet occupation of Lithuania. The local papers, of course, wrote nothing about this event. It was only when I returned to the United States that I found out that the name of this young patriot was Romas Kalanta. In subsequent visits to Kaunas after 1989, Fran and I were able to visit the memorial on the spot where he died so gruesomely.

From Riga we traveled to Moscow. There we visited many museums, walked through Red Square, visited Lenin's Mausoleum and his casket and many other notable places in Moscow. Some, reading these lines, will be astonished knowing that I, such a staunch and resolved anticommunist, would visit Red Square or Lenin's Mausoleum. The answer is very simple: art is art irrespective of where it was created and for what glorification. To tell the truth, I had no desire to see Stalin's grave, but this was part of the itinerary arranged by our guide. When we came to Stalin's grave I told the guide that I had no desire to see where he is buried. I was tempted to tell her a story about hell and suggest what to do with Stalin, but being an atheist, she probably would not have understood my desire.

The service in Moscow restaurants was terrible. In Lithuania and Latvia the service was considerably better, maybe because I was Lithuanian. With interest I noted the long lines of people everywhere. Our guide apparently had permission to take us places without standing in line, including the post office where I sent my father my dark suit. Later I was told that my father was buried in that suit. The only place where there were no lines was in the foreign currency stores, called "Beriozka," which in Russian means "a small birch tree". It was against the law for the local population to have hard currency, such as dollars, pound sterling or German marks. Consequently, there were not too many customers in the foreign currency stores. In fact, the Soviet people were forbidden to even enter these stores unless they were in the company of a foreign visitor.

Such foreign currency stores were in Vilnius, Riga, Moscow and Leningrad, now called St. Petersburg. There were stores, similar to the foreign currency stores, where high ranking Communist functionaries with special scripts could buy high quality local and foreign goods that were not available in the local stores. Such was life in the Communist "paradise" for over 90% of the population. (My description of the hard—foreign—currency and special stores is well known to most Lithuanians. However, this short description is dedicated to Americans that do not have an understanding about the "classless" society that the Communists were preaching.)

After Moscow we traveled for a few days to Leningrad (St. Petersburg). Seeing the museums and richly appointed buildings built by the czarist aristocracy left a deep impression on me. These stupendous and incredibly beautiful buildings from the outside and inside surely required many thousands of serfs to build and maintain. The well-restored and maintained museums attract many visitors including foreigners.

To punish believers, most churches in Lithuania, Latvia, Moscow, St. Petersburg and other cities of the former Soviet Union were converted into museums or warehouses. Restoring the beautiful, historic art treasures that were desecrated in the churches, synagogues and mosques will require a long time and much money.

From St. Petersburg we traveled to London with a short stop in Copenhagen, Denmark. In Copenhagen we were permitted to go out to the transit lounge where most of us immediately bought Western newspapers such as the London Times, the Wall Street Journal and other magazines. As soon as we began to leave the Soviet airplane in London, the stewardesses immediately began collecting the Western papers. It is difficult to describe the weight that left my shoulders after stepping off the plane on to free English soil. After a day in London we left for the United States— a few hours flight and we were home.

After exchanging the stories of our experience with our children and neighbors, I prepared to give speeches of my impressions to the Lithuanian community, and to write newspaper articles. I tried to be objective in describing life in Lithuania, Latvia and other Soviet countries, maybe even too objective  In 1977, when I submitted a request to go to Lithuania for a week to celebrate my parents 50th wedding anniversary, I received a very short answer from the Soviet Embassy. "Mr. Staciokas, your request for a visa is denied". When I asked why it was denied the answer was even shorter: "We are not obligated to explain".

Following my memorable visit, the time had come to start planning a new computer-related machine. Before launching such an undertaking I worked for a couple of months in the 1972 presidential election campaign.

## *Politics American Style*

In 1968, when I needed the local government permits to construct the building for our company, I had an opportunity to meet the Chester County Commission Chairman, Mr. Ted Rubino. I should note that in Pennsylvania the county commissioners, especially the chairmen, have great power in county government. Ted Rubino was not only the chairman of the county commissioners he also was the county Republican Party leader.

After I received the permit and became better acquainted with the commission chairman, we became reasonably good friends. His family immigrated to America from Italy and initially, like many immigrants, had difficulties making a living. Ted, being one of many children, remembered those hard times well. On some occasions we would discuss the difficulties of new immigrants and rejoiced that we had excellent opportunities in the United States to make a good living and maybe even save for old age. Politically we agreed because I was a registered Republican. I should mention that most Lithuanians that immigrated to the United States after the war were Republicans.

While we had high respect for President Roosevelt as a good domestic politician, we thought he was a poor statesman, who understood very little of international affairs—especially the villainous desires of Stalin, giving him and his murderous regime the eastern part of Europe and the Baltic States. The people of that part of Europe were left to bear the Communist yoke for over 54 years, because immediately after the war those parts of Europe were separated from Western Europe with an "iron curtain" that was lifted only after the freedom movements of 1989 in Eastern Europe.

After a period of time, Ted Rubino suggested that I run for the Pennsylvania State Senate and later maybe for the United States Congress. In those days the state senators worked only several months of the year and received rather small remuneration. In order to live decently they needed to have other income. Many of them were either lawyers or had businesses. Although I considered his suggestion as a personal honor, I declined, explaining that I did not know how to do two jobs adequately, that is, be a state senator and the president of a company.

I did not leave the political arena altogether and offered to help Ted Rubino a few hours a week as a volunteer. He thanked me and immediately offered me the position of treasurer for the new congressional candidate in our district. That was a very responsible position because the treasurer has to maintain accurate books for all political donations and, at the end of the campaign, send financial summaries to the state treasurer and the federal authorities. The treasurer could face jail time if they failed to maintain accurate accounting.

At the outset I decided to maintain honest and accurate books and refused to get involved in some questionable undertakings that occasionally surfaced in the political arena. The election was successful and our candidate won. We still had a substantial amount of money left in our treasury, which we could use in the next election in two years. As a reward, I was invited to Washington for the swearing-in ceremony for our congressman and the victory celebration where I met numerous congressmen and senators.

Two years later, in 1972, was the presidential election. The Republican Party chose President Nixon as their presidential candidate. That year there were no other candidates for the Republican nomination, which is generally the case with the sitting president. Each party has the presidential convention with a certain number of delegates from each state who gather in a selected city to nominate the candidate for the president and vice president. In Pennsylvania the Republican delegates were elected from congressional districts. I was offered the chance to be the candidate for delegate; I gladly accepted and was successfully elected. That was an honorary position and, if elected, one must pay his/her own way to the convention with no compensation of any kind. The Republican convention was held in Miami, Florida in August of 1972. There I had an opportunity to meet various US Government secretaries, many congressmen and senators, but the most memorable meeting was a dinner with President and Mrs. Nixon.

After several speeches and seminars about my experiences in Lithuania, I spent several months working on the campaigns for the United States president and my district congressman's elections. As a Republican Party delegate representing my district, I fulfilled my duty by voting for Nixon as the Republican candidate for United States president. After the convention I came back to Pennsylvania and began seriously planning to design a new computer-related machine—an electronic typewriter—and to start a new company.

## *Baltica Business Machines – My New Startup Company*

Planning and preliminary designs for the new machine took about four months. After finding the necessary engineers, technicians and renting the needed facilities, I started the new company with personal finances. After about six or seven months we needed additional financing which I was able to obtain from friends and business associates. The additional financing was needed to make further improvements in the product and to purchase equipment for production startup. At the end of 1973 we had a working prototype which we were able to demonstrate to potential investors.

In 1974 United States experienced economic difficulties. After the Yom Kippur war between Israel and the Arab countries, the Arabs imposed an oil embargo on the United States as vengeance

109

for our sympathy and the weapons we supplied to Israel. Later the Arabs doubled and even tripled the price of oil, not only to the United States but to Western European countries and Japan. As a result, there was an economic crisis in the highly industrialized countries.

Although the United States had domestic oil production that provided about half of our oil needs, the other half had to be imported primarily from Arab countries. The problem was compounded by the United States commitment to the Western European countries and Japan to provide low cost oil. This situation made it even more difficult to meet the domestic market needs of petroleum products such as gasoline, diesel and heating oil. Prices for these products skyrocketed and created lines at the gasoline pumps which had been unknown since the Second World War. Naturally the only industrial group that profited handsomely was the oil companies.

My new company needed substantial amounts of money for production equipment and to hire a production workforce. To secure bank loans was impossible. I was left with only one viable option and that was to find a buyer for the company. Sometime, during the summer of 1974, I found a buyer whose headquarters and production facility was in Florida. After the successful sale of my company, I and a few of my associates spent several months in Florida transferring the knowledge and documentation for our machine to the new owners.

The new owners offered me a job as vice president of European operations. Although the offer was very generous I declined, since I was required to live in Florida which was not to my liking. Shortly before Christmas 1974 I returned to Pennsylvania. Christmas and New Years passed very pleasantly. Although I did not have a job, I was not concerned because I knew that I would be able to get a job in the computer industry in the Philadelphia area.

In February of 1975 I received a very strange telephone call from an unknown person in New York. He suggested that we meet in New York at the Hilton Hotel at the potted palm tree to discuss potential opportunities in his company. He refused to reveal the company's name but assured me that the meeting is a serious matter, not a joke.

At that time I already had an offer as technology director in a division of Control Data Corporation (CDC) in Valley Forge, Pennsylvania, which was not too far from my home. The offer was good; a high salary and great options. I was supposed to start work there in two weeks. Since I had two weeks time I decided to go to New

York and find out something about this mysterious company. Actually it was my personal curiosity. Being 47 years old I was surprised to meet a 27-30-year-old bearded "junior" and his partner, an African-American about the same age. In my mind I wondered what kind of meeting this would be and mentally planned a civilized way to take leave as soon as possible.

Over the dinner they outlined a plan for an electronic typewriter, somewhat similar to the one that I sold to the Florida company. When it was my turn to talk I pointed out that to design and start production on such a machine would cost about $30 million. I also told them that such a large sum of money would be impossible to rise from friends, relatives or venture capitalists. I said that such undertaking would require a company with virtually inexhaustible financial resources that was prepared to spend a large amount of money coupled with a high risk. I explained to them that I knew only two types of industries that would be prepared to risk such sums of money: oil companies and gambling casinos. In my mind I dismissed the possibility that a computer or other high-technology company would send their representatives to talk to me without revealing their names.

They offered me a 9-12 month consulting agreement and handed me an already prepared document. On the letterhead of the consulting agreement I noted Exxon Corporation's name—the largest oil company in the world. One of their divisions, Exxon Enterprises, was responsible for high technology developments. Both of them smiled and asked me if I thought Exxon was a large enough corporation and able to risk such sums of money. I told them that Exxon is certainly a large enough concern and asked them if they were really committed. Their answer was: ABSO-LUTELY. I asked them why they contacted me. They said that their group, which was responsible for computer-related technologies development, knew about my electronic typewriter design and the sale to the Florida company. They regretted that Exxon did not get around in time to buy my designs.

Since I was not interested in a 9-12 month engagement, I asked them about Exxon Enterprises long term plans. The answer was not very complicated: if after 9-12 months I and a group of engineers could demonstrate the feasibility of an electronic typewriter, Exxon Enterprises would start a new division in which I would have high level responsibility with appropriate remuneration. I told the two men that I would get back to them and, after wishing them good night, went to bed.

The next day, after returning home, I thought

a lot and decided to take the risk with the Exxon Enterprises consulting job, exchanging guaranteed work at CDC for an uncertain future. Because I had experience in computer technology, I knew that if nothing developed with Exxon, I could always get a job in computer technology somewhere else.

## The Intelligent Typewriter

After completing the necessary documents and receiving guaranteed financing, I found suitable facilities and started the work. The first step was to find and engage the necessary engineers and technicians without revealing the source of financing. The work was started with a fictitious enterprise name—*LJS ASSOCIATES*, which are my initials.

Exxon Enterprises financial affairs were conducted in a manner that was strange even to someone like me who was used to unusual financial behavior. Once a month, after making a request, I received a wire transfer of the requested money to our bank. One day, I received a suggestion from Exxon Enterprise's vice president of finance to request larger sums of money covering several months of needs, because according to him, it was too much work for him to dribble small amounts every month. In his opinion, anything less than a million dollars was not worth his attention.

I accepted his offer and informed him that I would take any money that was not needed for a given month and purchase certificates of deposit and earn some interest. He told me flatly that investments were one of his responsibilities and I should keep the money in my checking account for which the bank paid no interest. My banker was very happy to keep a million dollars or more interest free for a few months. While we were developing the product, nobody checked my books or asked for financial summaries. Regardless, I decided to keep accurate books and register all expenses.

After eleven months, our engineers were able to demonstrate the feasibility of an electronic typewriter which satisfied Exxon Enterprises executives. At the end of that meeting in New York, myself and the "bearded young man," my partner, Dan Matthias, received permission to form a new division. The date was March 12, 1976. The new division was named "QYX," which are three meaningless letters, similar to a couple of other Exxon Enterprises divisions. Exxon liked such names because none of the languages of the world could attach any meaning to the letters—no country could find demeaning or belittling expressions in their languages based on the letters. Exxon had very strong feelings about possible insults to other countries because the company conducted business in most of the world.

On the way from New York to Pennsylvania we decided that the new division headquarters would be close to my home. We also divided the duties as follows: Dan Matthias would be the president of the division because he had close ties with Exxon Enterprises management in New York while I would be senior vice president and chief operating officer. That same day I informed our coworkers, who were the financial backers of the enterprise, of the changes. Everybody was delighted and understood that a strong company like Exxon would provide the necessary financing for such a huge enterprise.

After finding a larger facility, we started looking for more engineers and other workers with various necessary skills. This time I did not need to worry about the various documents, for they were being handled by my partner Dan Matthias along with Exxon attorneys and their vice president of finance. I, therefore, had a free hand to start the design and development of the electronic typewriter. We named the future new machine the *"INTELLIGENT TYPEWRITER"*.

Our new machine required many inventions to produce: low cost microprocessors, a low profile storage device, a small power supply, magnetic levitation for the carriage and several other inventions that were not in existence at the time. After seven months we had over 30 engineers, software writers and technicians on the job. We all worked over 10 hours per day, six days a week compared to eight hours per day and five days a week in other industries. Morale was very high and all wanted to succeed.

After about 15 months, in August of 1977, we had several electronic typewriter prototypes built by our engineers and technicians, which were used for various experiments with not the best results. Some of these prototypes were placed in Exxon offices in New York and in our laboratories. When those machines failed, the secretaries were not too enthusiastic to continue using them. Dan Matthias spent a lot of time in New York trying to convince the secretaries to continue using our typewriters. Sometimes he even had to bribe them with candies and flowers. In the meantime we were sweating in the laboratory.

Here I will depart from the main subject and cover a personal event. In mid-1977, we had about 15 coworkers and needed secretarial help. We put an advertisement for a secretary in a local newspaper. Several ladies answered our advertisement. It was my responsibility to interview them.

117

One of the candidates came with laryngitis and could hardly talk. That lady was Fran, my future wife. She had good experience and it seemed that she wanted the job more than the others. Later I found out that she lived less than a mile from our laboratory while her job at the time was about 35 miles away. After checking out her recommendations and verifying her qualifications, we offered her a job. She agreed and after two weeks started work, sharing difficulties with the engineers testing the new Intelligent Typewriter.

After the interviews, I kidded my coworkers that I finally found a woman who will not talk back to me because she can hardly talk. Their joking comment was that this is only a womanish trick and I better watch out. At that time I did not think that the time would come when I would have to listen to her not only during the day but at night as well. We started dating March 10, 1978 and after six years, on March 10, 1984 we were married.

In the fall of 1977, we began planning for mass production. Our plans were such that in the summer of 1978 we would reach a yearly production rate of 80,000 units. Therefore, we needed a 300,000-square-foot production facility. After reaching our target rate, we would need over 1,000 coworkers. Exxon is a firm believer in owning the facilities and suggested that we do the same. We needed to find over 10 acres of ground where we could house a single story building that was our target size and had sufficient parking spaces. The building plans, finding the necessary ground, agreements with potential building contractors and the necessary permits took a lot of my time. I worked over 10 hours per day because the planning of the building required almost eight hours, and I still wanted to know what was going on in the laboratory. After finalizing the plans and turning over the work to the building contractors, I finally was able to join my coworkers who were planning the announcement, display and demonstration of our Intelligent Typewriter.

All the plans and work required extraordinary efforts not only from me but also from the over 200 coworkers we had at the time. Although we worked hard, on certain occasions we managed to have a party for the workers and their families. The company paid for such parties which helped to maintain high morale for the workers and satisfaction for the families.

The building work progressed well, particularly since my partner paid special attention to the young, good looking lady architect. After a couple of years they got married and currently live in Philadelphia, Pennsylvania.

In late January 1978 we traveled to New Orleans, Louisiana for the office equipment conference and product exhibition. The demonstrations of our new typewriter went very well. Our exhibition booth was "five rows deep," and attracted not only visitors, but a large press contingent as well. The interest in our Intelligent Typewriter was twofold. First, the product was the first of such high technical innovation, while the second was that Exxon Corporation financed the venture.

During the press conferences I had to answer many questions to members of other companies and news media representatives. Our technical achievements meant that other companies in office products business such as IBM, UNIVAC, Xerox and others were left far behind. We were determined to expand the mass production of the Intelligent Typewriter the fastest possible way, because we knew that these other companies, having large technical and manufacturing capabilities, would eventually develop and produce competing products. It was just a matter of time and it was not long in coming.

# $\mathcal{C}$hapter VII

## Exxon: Domestic and
## Overseas Expansion

According to Exxon Enterprises instructions we had to market and sell the Intelligent Typewriter directly from our own sales offices. All sales offices had to be the same size, design and contain the same decorations. During the first year we opened 24 sales offices in the largest cities of the United States. After about one year our sales were going well, however, all sales offices were still losing money. The opening of sales offices, hiring and training of marketing and sales support staff was costing us about $500,000 per office. We planned, that after two years of operation each office would have to be profitable. In many offices this was achieved, but several offices required changes including new office managers.

Unfortunately, after about two years, many of our direct sales offices were not reaching sales goals. In the meantime, based on sales projections, we had about 10,000 Intelligent Typewriters in the warehouse. There was no choice but to try to sell through distributors in the United States. With the help of our sister company Vydec, we established relationships with over 30 office product dealers in the smaller cities of United States, where we had no direct sales offices. This decision proved to be very fortuitous because, within six to nine months, our dealers were outselling our direct office in volume profit.

After starting our sales of the Intelligent Typewriter in the United States, we began to plan sales expansion abroad. We decided to start sales in Australia because we were concerned that by opening sales in any European country we would have a gray market in neighboring countries. Australia, being an eight-hour plane flight away from another large industrial country, Japan, would not likely cause illegal sales of our product. The other important consideration was that Australia uses the English language and therefore, the technical changes to the Intelligent Typewriter were minimal.

During the planning stages for overseas sales, we decided to use distributors instead of our own sales offices abroad. This was done primarily for economic and cultural reasons. We understood that in some countries, such as Germany, an established local office products company can do a better and faster job of sales than a new American subsidiary.

## *Expanding to Australia*

After reaching an agreement with an Australian computer and office products sales and marketing company, we began preparations for an announcement and advertising in the city of Sydney. It was my responsibility to open the show and give interviews to the news media. The introductory show was held in the world-renown opera house in Sydney's harbor. The opera house's architecture is very unique, probably the only one of its kind in the world. Looking at it from a distance it appears as if the building, with its sails, is floating on the water. To me personally, Sidney Bay and harbor is one of the most beautiful bays of the six that I am familiar with, namely Acapulco, Mexico; Naples and Venice, Italy; Hong Kong, China and the Principality of Monaco.

The opening of the product show produced excellent results. There was great interest in our Intelligent Typewriter resulting in many orders, while I, in the meantime, had to spend over two hours answering reporters' questions.

During the three years that I was associated with the Australian distributor, I made about ten trips to several cities in that wonderful country and met a lot of great people. I had an opportunity to associate with more than 20 people and visit the vastness of the Australian Outback that starts about 200 miles beyond Sydney. The farmers in the Outback raise mostly sheep on thousands of acres of grazing land, with neighbors living several hundred miles from each other. Some weekends, these "neighbors" gather together, visiting each other using small planes. Australians are very hospitable and generous people, and many have interesting views. They take pride in the fact that their ancestors were British convicts that were exiled to Australia, which in the nineteenth century was a British possession. The other interesting view is that when an Australian says he or she is going home for a holiday, it means he/she is going to visit London, England. It is unimportant that their ancestors had not lived in England for several generations.

### Opening Business in Great Britain

The next foreign country where we opened distribution was Great Britain. Our central sales and marketing office was located in London. The question arose why Great Britain and not another major European country. The answer is simple; our Intelligent Typewriter was in English, therefore we needed to make very few changes to accommodate British English. After opening our office and providing demonstrations of our product in London we were very quickly able to satisfy the product demand in Great Britain. During the opening of our office and display of our products, I again had to give interviews to the news media and answer question that were similar to the questions in Australia. By now I had an easier time during interviews because, so to speak, I had experience in associating with reporters and the business leaders of London and other major cities of Great Britain.

The United Kingdom is very interesting because it is the oldest continuous reigning kingdom in the world. The royal family has no ruling powers, which are vested in the Prime Minister. The royalty is the tradition and moral force dating back to the twelfth century. The royalty is revered almost like a religion and even when the Communists had some voice, they did not dare to criticize the crown. It is a spectacle to see the changing of the guards at Buckingham Palace. The guards, as far as I have heard, have no ammunition in their rifles, wear very imposing uniforms and the change routine is ancient custom. The real security of the palace is in the hands of the police.

I know London very well, because from the middle of 1981 until 1985 I spent a great deal of time in Great Britain and particularly in London. (About that I will write later.)

## Opening of Sales Office in Germany

While planning for the startup of business in Germany I received an invitation to give a paper at the German Engineer's Day in Nuremberg on May 29-31, 1979. The paper was very technical because our Intelligent Typewriter contained several inventions that were of interest to engineers of several high technology capable countries.

I decided to give the talk in German. During the question and answer period I did not want to share much of still highly confidential information, therefore I advised the gathering that my German was inadequate to answer some complex technical questions and requested that the questions be addressed in English. I thought that I would have a limited number of simple questions in English by a few individuals who may have mastered the English language, but I was mistaken. I was surprised when over 400 hands went up and the questions were in very fluent English. So ended my "clever" ruse and I was obligated to answer the questions in English. This confirmed again the high standards in German universities, particularly in technical subjects.

At the end of the day Fran and I were invited to a dinner and a round-table discussion regarding technologies in the United States and in particular, technologies employed in the development of the Intelligent Typewriter. Fran was seated between two German engineers who spoke English fluently and I had to answer questions to all seated at the table; so much for the "round table" discussions. Although by the questions, I was being lead to answer some highly confidential company information, I managed to elude disclosing confidential information due to my earlier experiences in the previous interviews. The evening passed very pleasantly. Fran and I talked for many months about our experiences during the German Engineer's Day.

After returning to the United States we finalized plans to open the German market. Earlier we decided that we would make a German Intelligent Typewriter, which meant that the typewriter keys, alphabet, all visible signs and instructions would be in German.

In the early fall of 1979 we opened several sales offices with headquarters in Hamburg, because that is where our partner's main office was. Here again, after the opening ceremonies and demonstrations I was required to give interviews to the news media and the representatives of many German industries. Our German partner organized everything extremely well and consequently, the opening went very well. Fran and I spent a pleasant week in Germany. The sales in Germany proceeded extremely well and after about a year the German sales were about twice those of Great Britain and Australia.

### *Business Expansion in Other Countries*

After the successful opening of German markets the time had come to expand in other European countries. The next country was France, a little later Switzerland and Austria. I was asked many times what made us select the countries in this order.

If we wished to sell products in France it was necessary to have a French language Intelligent Typewriter. Having German and French language typewriters it was easy to market such products in Switzerland, where about 90% of the Swiss people speak German and French. Austria uses the German language, therefore, while doing business in Germany, it was easy to enter the Austrian market with the German language Intelligent Typewriter.

Canada, the United State's northern neighbor,

uses the English and French languages therefore it was easy to start sales of our English and French products. After designing our products in the Spanish and Italian languages, time had come to plan business expansion in the Far East and South America. After about nine months, in the later part of 1980, we had sales branches in Japan, Hong Kong and Singapore.

Having a Spanish language typewriter it was easy to expand our business in South America, because with the exception of Brazil and a few other small countries, all the rest of the South and Central American states use the Spanish language. We did not have our branches in South America therefore we decided to use sales agents.

At the beginning of 1981 we had either sales branches or sales agents in more than 25 countries in Western Europe, Asia, Australia, North, South and Central America, the Near East and several African countries. We had no plans to do business with the Communist countries including the Soviet Union. In the middle of 1981, we became aware that our Intelligent Typewriter was known and being used in Moscow, Warsaw and Budapest. We knew how our products were sold and shipped to the Soviet Union, Poland and Hungary, but could do nothing about stopping such unwanted business, where we had no sanctioned representation.

## My Travels

During the expansion of our business, I traveled to most of the countries where we were doing business giving seminars, interviews and meeting local business people. I was very intrigued with Spain. At one time Spain was the largest world empire that ruled over most of South and Central America, the Caribbean Island basin, the Philippine Islands and even some parts of today's United States. One should stop and think how such a powerful country, that for over 300 years ruled over large parts of the world, transporting gold, silver and other wealth home to Spain, is so poor today. The wealth that Spain accumulated was wasted on loosing wars, poor management of the country and almost nonexistent statesmanship. Indeed, in the twentieth century Spain almost went broke, had a devastating civil war, and only in the past two decades, after becoming a member of the European Union, it began to recover economically.

History teaches us how powerful empires, such as Spain, Rome, Ottoman Turkey, Portugal, Czarist and Communist Russia, the old Chinese Empire, Austro-Hungary, the Polish-Lithuanian Kingdom and some other collapsed empires went bankrupt. This happened because of poor internal and foreign policies, corruption, treason, the moral decay of the government, suppression of their citizen's rights and a huge discrepancy in the distribution of wealth between the rulers and the ruled. It would be desirable that Lithuanian politicians and some other country's leaders recently freed from the communist yoke would study and learn from history's lessons.

In Spain there are some well cared-for old beautiful churches—the Spaniards are deeply religious Roman Catholics. One Spanish peculiarity is bull fights. There are arenas exclusively for bull fighting while the bullfighters (toreadors) are treated as sports celebrities. Spaniards are fanatical about this sport, if one can call it that, even more than Germans and Britons are to soccer. I have seen a few bullfights but cannot say that I liked them; I went merely to be polite to my Spanish hosts. This Spanish sport is also practiced in some South American countries that at one time were Spanish colonies.

The country that I was very impressed with was Singapore. It is a small island, in reality a city state with over two million people that is connected via bridge to Malaysia. It is a very orderly, clean and safe city. The population is composed of over 50% Chinese, about 25% Indians, about 10% English that stayed there after the end of British colonialism and another 15% Indonesians. With all the different cultures and religions, the people get along with each other remarkably well. The official language is English, although the people use their native languages. I visited there a couple of weeks when we opened our sales office. During introductions I gave a technical- and business-related talk and received a very warm reception. During the past fifteen years my wife and I have visited Singapore several times and enjoyed every visit.

Another country that I had the pleasure to visit for potential business was Israel. Just getting into Israel in 1980 was an experience that today we encounter every day in every country of the world—security. Before boarding the plane from Geneva, Switzerland to Israel my wife and I had to undergo a total security check which consisted of the following: Our luggage had to be opened and inspected by the Israeli security representatives. The luggage then was deposited at the entrance to the plane. Before boarding the plane we were required to identify our luggage which was then placed on the plane. After our arrival at Ben Gurion Airport in Tel Aviv we had to go through another very thorough screening, where passport control agents asked a variety of questions, some of which had nothing to do with our travel plans. At that time we did not know that the trained immigration agents were searching for clues for persons that could do harm to Israel. That is why to this day Israel is the most capable country in deterring terrorists.

Our host was very gracious and accommodating to our needs. After discussing the potential of selling the Intelligent Typewriter to the Israeli market, he took us to Jerusalem, showed us the notable places in town and explained to us some of the history of Jerusalem. He also arranged a personal guide to lead us through the Via Delarosa—the way of the Cross for Jesus—from the palace of Pontius Pilot to Golgotha, the hill near Jerusalem where Jesus was crucified. Today there is a church with various Christian denominations claiming the rights to oversee the property. Needless to say, my wife and I were moved by the experience of stepping on the ground that Jesus walked on and experienced his suffering. This was a journey for both which we will never forget.

At the beginning of 1981 Exxon Enterprises decided to unite their three independent technical entities ostensibly to minimize overhead costs. I was offered the position of vice president of European operations in the new entity. I would have had to live in Switzerland for a couple of years which to me was not a very attractive option. I also thought that the expansion of the European headquarters operations was an unnecessary and costly undertaking. Consequently I declined the offer.

# $\mathcal{C}$hapter VIII

## COMTECH, PLC

On June 29 or 30, 1981 I received a very peculiar telephone call from a European who spoke good English, inviting me to meet him at the Philadelphia airport to discuss an opportunity to work with a European entity whose name he declined to give me over the phone. The individual assured me that this was a serious proposition and said that it would be worth my while to meet him and discuss this European possibility.

Because the Philadelphia airport was only about 30 miles from my home, the curiosity of this peculiar circumstance led me to agree to meet him. The meeting was very formal with real European manners displayed by the gentleman. During the conversation it became clear that he was a "head hunter" located in Geneva, Switzerland. He was engaged by a British oil company to find a leader for a not-yet-formed but planned high technology enterprise. After some more discussions it became apparent that he knew a great deal about me personally and my experience. He invited me to come to Geneva, Switzerland that weekend to meet several board members of this oil company. Because it was the Fourth of July weekend, I tried to delay the travel, but he finally convinced me to come to Geneva that weekend.

That Friday morning, in the Geneva airport, I was met by the same gentleman that I had discussions with in Philadelphia and another individual, a Swiss national, Mr. Jean-Robert Bugnion, who also spoke fluent English. After a short ride in a car, we wound up in the very expensively appointed office of TRICENTRAL OIL CO, LTD. My immediate thought was, here again, I am getting involved with another oil company. After very formal introductions we began the discussions. Two members of the board, Misters Dennis Hulbert and Peter Moody, questioned me rather superficially and I came to the conclusion that they knew very little about technology. Mr. Bugnion had a better understanding about the technology, although his specialty was finance.

For lunch they took me to a very expensive restaurant which I knew from my earlier travel to Geneva. The lunch lasted about two hours with excellent food, wine and deserts. I silently thought that they tried to convey the abundance of the company and impress me with such an expensive lunch. After lunch, I finally got an opportunity to meet the chairman of the board, Mr. James George Stoddart Longcroft III, a real high-class British subject.

The interview was conducted with just the two of us in his office. He told me a lot about himself, how he became associated with the oil company and that recently he spun off the non-oil business of Tricentral Oil Co. and named the new company COMTECH, PLC. This new company already had two technology-related divisions and an automobile dealership. He explained to me that Comtech had a technical association with a high technology development company in England not far from London. He asked me to visit that technology development company and give my assessment about two new products that were being developed there with Comtech financing. If I had an affirmative impression about the products he wanted to know if it would be worth it to start production of those products in the United States.

He admitted that he and the board members of Comtech knew very little about technology.

I agreed to go to England because I was already in Switzerland and my weekend was already lost. I traveled to England late that evening after dinner with one of the members of the board, Mr. Moody. I spent the night in a rather expensive hotel, which unbeknown to me at that time would become my "home away from home" whenever I was in the United Kingdom. (About that I will write later.)

The following day, Mr. Moody and I traveled by train to Cambridge to visit that development company. I was introduced to several engineers and the general manager of the organization. I must say that I was favorably impressed with the engineers and especially the general manager, Mr. Gordon Edge, who understood technology well and spoke very eloquently, almost with the salesmanship flair, about the company and its product development. I got the impression that he could sell an icebox to an Eskimo!

After having seen the development and demonstrations of the two products for Comtech, and having a chance to talk to some engineers and ask questions, I decided that I had enough understanding to give my assessment to Mr. Longcroft. Before leaving the Cambridge laboratories, Mr.

Edge offered me the opportunity to visit their facility in New Jersey and said that he would be there the following week. I thanked him for the detailed information about the products and promised to visit him in New Jersey. Late in the afternoon Mr. Moody and I left Cambridge for London and the following day I flew back to the United States.

After several days home, I went to visit Mr. Edge and his laboratories in New Jersey where I had a tour and some more discussions with Mr. Edge. I formed an opinion that he was too optimistic about the development of the new products and converting them so quickly into commercial successes. He asked me what I thought about the commercial potential of the Comtech products. I told him honestly that there were possibilities for the products, but not as soon as he and the engineers thought. I told him, that by my judgment, there were still many areas that required considerable development time. I could sense that Mr. Edge was not too thrilled about my opinion regarding the development status of the two products for Comtech.

The following day I called Mr. Longcroft and told him my assessment about the development status and potential commercial success of the two products. He immediately suggested that we meet in New York at the airport the following day and talk more about the company plans.

After describing to Fran my travel experiences in Switzerland and England and the phone conversation with Mr. Longcroft, I said the next day would be decisive. In fact that is exactly how it happened. During the meeting with Mr. Longcroft, I summarized my findings in Cambridge, my opinion about potential commercialization of those products, and the time to finalize the development and opening of a factory in United States.

He asked me several questions and I finally found out what he had in mind. He immediately offered me the position of the president of this new division, a position on the board not only in the new division but board membership in Comtech and that I would immediately take over oversight of product development in Cambridge. The salary, the stock options in the new division and in Comtech and other perks were quite generous. He also suggested that not only the factory, but the product development laboratory also should be in the United States.

I asked him where the money would come from for such an undertaking. He answered that as soon as I confirm my acceptance of the job offer, he would transfer about 12 million dollars for the new division to a designated bank in the United States. All conditions were acceptable to me except membership on the Comtech board. I tried to explain to him that forming the new division and overseeing the product development in Cambridge would be more than enough work for me. He insisted that I take the board seat in Comtech because I would be the only member of the board with technical qualifications and knowledge. Finally, after considerable discussion, I agreed to take a seat on the Comtech board in addition to all the other duties. He promised to send me the job offer in writing and wished me good luck in the new job.

When I came back from New York, I discussed my offer with Fran and told her that the day after I received the offer in writing I would turn in my resignation to Qyx, division of Exxon Enterprises. I did not need to wait long. After two days I received the job offer in writing from Mr. Longcroft. Writing the resignation letter was a very difficult step for me because my Qyx coworkers and Exxon Enterprises executives had a high level of confidence in me. The president of the Qyx division arranged a very excellent going-away party for me and as a gift gave me a new Intelligent Typewriter with the following inscription: *Leon Staciokas, Sr. Vice President for his entrepreneurship and dedication to Qyx.*

On the first of September 1981, I started my

new job in the Comtech division that had no name yet. The first step was a trip to the Comtech headquarters in London, where I was officially installed as a new member of the Comtech board. Following that, the board ratified the new division and my job as the president of that division. About a month later the new division had a name, which was MNEMOS. The name was based on Greek mythology where Mnemosyne and the god Zeus had nine daughters, each of whom presided over arts and sciences. The daughter Muse was a guiding spirit, a source of inspiration.

The same day, the Comtech secretary arranged for my stay in the Britannia Hotel in London's elite district, Grosvenor Square, near the American embassy. Here was my "home away from home" for about two-and-a-half-years, because I had to travel to London at least once a month and was spending about a week or more each time. Fran visited me several times and we had an opportunity to visit notable places in London.

London was started by the Romans about 40 A.D. as a defense fortification. To this day there are a few walls that the Romans built still standing. London experienced a tremendous destruction during the German air raids, but now the city is rebuilt with no traces of the destruction. The notable places to visit are the Parliament Building, St.

Paul's Cathedral, numerous museums and parks, Piccadilly Circus, Trafalgar Square, London Tower and Buckingham Palace.

## New Comtech Division: "MNEMOS"

When I came back to the United States after travels in London, I had to find engineers, technicians and other skilled workers. For insurance purposes the health checkup for the first eight workers took place at Fran's house because the company did not yet have its own facilities. We decided to locate our headquarters near Princeton, New Jersey because of the availability of skilled software engineers and the proximity to Princeton University, with its library and professors who were available for consulting. In addition, it was a reasonably short distance to the Newark and New York airports, an advantage since we knew that we would have to travel extensively to Europe. The only undesirable part of the transition was relocating our residence from Pennsylvania to New Jersey. Since Fran was my partner/helper in the formation of the company Mnemos, she agreed to move to New Jersey.

After those decisions, I again had to travel to London, so I asked Fran to find the company headquarters facility and a house for us somewhere near Princeton. When, after more than a

143

week in London, I came back to the United States, Fran had already found the facilities for the company and a house for us.

When I agreed to form the new Comtech division and relocate the development laboratory and production facility from the United Kingdom to the United States, I knew that it would take a lot of work, but I did not know how much. I had to oversee the development of two products in Cambridge, England, find a facility in the London area for our European sales and marketing staff and find suitable workers in the United Kingdom and the United States. In addition to all this work I also had to fulfill the duties as a member of the board of Comtech that required two or three days per month.

Not too long after joining Comtech I found out that Mr. Longcroft was very much against paying any taxes to any government. He moved his residence from England to Switzerland where there was no unearned income and no inheritance taxes. He absolutely insisted to register Mnemos in Bermuda, which although being a British colony did not have corporate profit tax. He also wanted to avoid paying possible taxes on potential patent royalties by registering patents in the Netherlands Antilles. When we finally finished all the necessary documentation, our company Mnemos had

18 different registration documents located in the United States, the United Kingdom, Liechtenstein, Luxemburg, Bermuda, Netherlands Antilles and Curacao in the West Indies, Caribbean.

I expressed my opinion regarding these convoluted, complex and unnecessarily expensive registrations to Mr. Longcroft. I pointed out that each of these countries required yearly registration maintenance fees, albeit relatively small sums of money. However, in order to avoid our United States registration to look like a sham, we had to establish Mnemos, a bona fide residence in Bermuda and all annual financial reporting had to be prepared in Bermuda. We had to relocate our controller to Bermuda and rent an apartment there, which was very expensive compared to United States housing. In addition, we also were required by Bermudian law to have two Bermuda citizens as members of Mnemos' board. With all the facts in hand I was unable to change Mr. Longcrot's mind. In general, the only value that I personally derived from these machinations was that I learned the ways of various countries' business registrations and the European view regarding corporate and personal income taxes.

As soon as I started working, I recognized that the plan created by Mr. Moody with his associates and assisted by Mr. Edge from Pathcentre, the technology consulting firm, for starting production of the two products, or more accurately systems, was much too optimistic. For starters, I had to convince the Comtech board that we could not continue the development of the two products simultaneously because both products required several material and technological inventions. I expressed an opinion that to finish both product designs we would run out of money before being able to start production. I stated that in my technical judgment and my engineers' evaluations during their visit to Cambridge Pathcentre laboratories, we could not start production as planned earlier, because the products were only in the engineering prototype feasibility demonstration stage. The problem was that the earlier team members, with Mr. Moody's agreement, began purchasing parts for initial production. I had to inform Mr. Longcroft that it was a mistake to purchase any parts at this stage. I also told him and the Comtech board that we would have to scrap all parts on hand and write off any other commitments that existed.

Mr. Moody, who like myself was a member of the Comtech board, and had a very close relationship with Mr. Edge of Pathcentre, expressed dissatisfaction with my recommendation and tried to convince me to change my mind. He even tried to imply that perhaps I did not adequately understand the technology and should reconsider my position. I told him frankly that this was an insult to mine and my American engineers' technical competence and I should bring this issue to the Comtech board. He immediately apologized stating that we did not need a board meeting but rather the three of us, himself, me and Mr. Edge should get together and discuss the issue.

The meeting of the three of us, Mr. Moody, Mr. Edge and myself, decided the issue to my favor. Mr. Edge admitted that perhaps he was rushing to start production, but insisted that from the technical standpoint there were no unresolved problems. I pointed out that in my judgment, there were a number of technical issues that would need to be resolved and would take about a year of research and development before any one of the two products would be ready to start production. The events proved that my judgment was correct, because it took about a year of concerted engineering effort to bring one of these products to the initial production stage. Although I was right, my relationship with Mr. Moody was correct only in official business. I did not trust him for he had shifty eyes and had difficulty looking you straight in the face when talking.

I am certain Mr. Moody was not too overjoyed with my presence, but had to tolerate me because I had the confidence of the chairman Mr. Longcroft who was satisfied with my work.

At the beginning of 1982, our consulting firm Pathcentre expanded their facilities. Prince Philip, Queen Elizabeth's husband, was invited for the opening ceremonies of the new building. Because I was in London at that time, I had an opportunity to shake hands with the prince and explain some of the technologies of our products. There are opinions not only in the United States, but in some other countries as well, that Prince Philip is a dunce with limited intelligence. After talking to him for about 15 minutes, I would like to state categorically that Prince Philip possesses extraordinary intelligence, speaks eloquently and has a good grasp of modern technology. I would like to remind the readers that this man was the captain of a British warship and also piloted fighter planes and helicopters. With limited intelligence, even being from the royal house, one could not possibly achieve such deeds.

Around March of 1982 we began to move technical information and documentation from Cambridge, England to our laboratories in Princeton, New Jersey. Our technical work proceeded according to earlier established plans. By September of 1982 we began demonstrations of our System 6000 to selected potential customers in the

United States and Europe. Because the System 6000 was complicated with large specialized software, we needed not only sales people but also technical support staff who operated as a team during customer demonstrations and technical explanations. We anticipated that it would take about a year after demonstrations before we received an order and it would take another year before the System 6000 was operational at the customer's site. Sales efforts and demonstrations were made in the United States, the United Kingdom, France, Germany, Belgium and Italy. I had to travel to these countries and tried to convince potential customers about the quality and value of our system.

We calculated that MNEMOS would incur losses for the next two years and began to worry about how to get additional working capital. We decided to register MNEMOS on the London Stock Exchange. Although I was familiar with stock exchanges in the United States, the London Stock Exchange operated somewhat differently than the New York Stock Exchange and I had to learn some new things. It took a couple of months to prepare the necessary documents and prospectus according to the London Stock Exchange requirements. During those two months, I spent most of the time in the London hotel and in the lawyers and underwriters offices. Finally, the day of the registration of MNEMOS on the London Stock Exchange arrived. We successfully sold part of the company and received about 14-million dollars which had to cover operating expenses for the following two years, until we received income from the sale of the first System 6000.

At the beginning of 1983 our chairman, Mr. Longcroft, decided to move Comtech and all its divisions' headquarters to Vevey, Switzerland. He did that to avoid paying corporate income taxes, although at that time only the automobile sales and service division TRIMOCO was profitable. His wishes probably were influenced by the fact that his home in Gstaat was about 20 miles away from Vevey. I thought that this move was an unnecessary waste of money but he had majority votes on the board, so I had to go along with the decision.

After a couple of months we had a first board meeting of Comtech and all its divisions in Vevey, Switzerland. Vevey, situated on the banks of Lake Geneva, is a picture postcard city. It is a typical Swiss city, very clean, orderly and over seven hundred years old. The world famous chocolate and food concern Nestle has its headquarters in Vevey. For a long time, movie star Charlie Chaplin lived in Vevey. Several times I had an opportunity to visit Chaplin's beloved restaurant that occupied a house built in the fourteenth century. In Vevey

I lived through several interesting, difficult and complicated situations.

After about a year we received our first order for System 6000 with certain requirements for which we did not have the technology. Again we had to do additional development work. Reading technical journals and talking to our engineers, I began to wonder if our technology was too old for the market that we were addressing. After doing additional analysis and investigations, I was compelled to tell the Comtech board that we probably would need new technology in place of the current one. These changes would require additional development and would delay sales of the new technology System 6000. The new technology consisted of a CD-ROM in place of an analog recording of data on a flexible disk.

The opportunity arrived for Mr. Moody to suggest to the board that I had lost confidence in the current technology and perhaps someone else, namely himself with the help of Mr. Edge, could continue to exploit the current technology. After long and stormy discussions within the board, I offered to resign as president of MNEMOS and as a member of the MNEMOS board. Mr. Moody immediately volunteered that he could temporarily take over the presidency of MNEMOS. The next day Mr. Longcroft agreed with my proposition and asked that I stay on the Comtech board and to take the position of deputy chairman of the board of another Comtech division, LASER-STORE, which was located near Philadelphia.

When after a few days I came home, I told Fran what I had done and she agreed with my decision, although from her face I could tell she was not too overjoyed. The next morning I called a meeting of MENMOS coworkers and told them about my resignation and Mr. Moody's temporary appointment as president. Later I found out that the workers of MNEMOS were not happy with my resignation and Mr. Moody taking over my duties. Some predicted dire difficulties in the future. Their prophecies came to pass over the next six months. Mr. Moody wasted money various ways including engaging Mr. Edge as a consultant to help him with technology issues. After about a year the money was gone and technologically MNEMOS fell behind even further.

The chairman, Mr. Longcroft, sensed that something was going wrong in MNEMOS and asked me to join MNEMOS board. After writing a long and detailed report regarding MNEMOS technology and the prospects for the future, I agreed to join MNEMOS board.

As I detailed in my report, the CD-ROM technology was expanding rapidly while MNEMOS technology was falling further behind. We needed to find a solution for MNEMOS financial situation. We decided to sell the division to a group of venture capitalists. The leader of this group asked me to stay on the board after the sale, but did not ask Mr. Moody to remain on the board. Later I found out in a round-about way that Mr. Moody was very unhappy about not being invited to join the new board, which did not matter to me at all— I did not care about his unhappiness. MNEMOS name was changed to IS/R (**I**nformation **S**torage/ **R**etrieval) System in late 1985. I remained on the Board of IR/S Systems until 1990 when I resigned because of the demands in my job at a new company.

## *Liquidating LASERSTORE*

As a member of the board of IS/R Systems and a member of the Comtech board, I continued to work as deputy chairman of LASERSTORE. Somehow fate dealt me a hand where I had to make an assessment of the commercial viability of LASERSTORE and report my finding to the Comtech board. In the middle of 1986 I decided that LASERSTORE had no commercial possibilities because its technology was too complicated and there were substitutes in the market which were simpler and less costly. I suggested to the

Comtech board to sell the division. I should point out that the LASERSTORE technology was developed by Pathcentre under Mr. Egde's guidance. My "coworker" on the board, Mr. Moody, did not agree with my recommendation and suggested continued further development work in LASERSTORE, perhaps with his assistance. This time Mr. Longcroft did not agree with Mr. Moody and told him to sell the division. I was instructed to take over the management of LASERSTORE and pursue liquidation if the sale was not successful.

After three or four months I recommended to the Comtech board to liquidate LASERSTORE, because during that time Mr. Moody did not receive a single offer for the purchase of the division. During the next three months I liquidated the LASERSTORE division.

# Chapter IX

## IOMEGA Corporation

In February of 1987 I got in contact with Mr. Dave Dunn, who was the chairman of the board of Iomega Corporation and a man I had previously known. He told me that the company was looking for a vice president of operations. He also told me that Mr. Kucha, who was a member of the Board, and currently serving as temporary president of Iomega, would get in touch with me soon. Indeed, after a few days I received a telephone call from Mr. Kucha, who suggested that we meet in Boston. During the meeting in Boston he outlined for me the current difficulties in Iomega and said that he would get in touch with Mr. Dunn. He also told me that "if everything goes as planned" I would be interviewed by several members of the board.

The following week I had interviews with three members of the board and several days later, received a telephone call from Mr. Dunn inviting me to come to San Diego, where he lived, for an interview with him. I traveled there with just a briefcase expecting the next day to be back in Pennsylvania. After a long discussion and lunch, he called Mr. Kucha in Roy, Utah and while I was sitting there, suggested that Mr. Kucha make a deal with me. So instead of going back to Pennsylvania, I traveled to Utah for more interviews with some of the Iomega managers and Mr. Kucha. After spending almost all day together, Mr. Kucha and I reached an agreement regarding my salary, stock options, relocation expenses, sign-on bonus and a few other minor details. He promised within a few days to send me an offer letter. After I signed the acceptance letter and sent it back to him, I would become an Iomega employee—sr. vice president of operations—with the following departments reporting to me: R&D, manufacturing, quality and facilities. After returning home, Fran and I discussed the offer and the risks involved, because at that time Iomega had many difficulties. We both agreed for me to take the position at Iomega, but she would remain in Pennsylvania for at least six months because of the uncertainties with Iomega's business situation. I signed the offer letter and started to work at Iomega.

## Shaking up the Operations

According to company documents, I started work at Iomega on August 13, 1987 as senior vice president of operations. However, my auto trip from Philadelphia to Roy, Utah covering about 2,300 miles took almost three days—time counted as working time. Therefore, in reality, my first working day was Monday, August 17.

The basic Iomega product was the Bernoulli Box, which was a removable magnetic storage disk drive that could be connected to a PC (Personal Computer) or Macintosh desk top computer. The disks were eight inches and 5-1/4 inches in diameter and could store from 10 to 44 megabytes of data.

Iomega developed products using flexible magnetic media that were based on fluid dynamics technology that was explained in the eighteenth century by Swiss mathematician Daniel Bernoulli.

The first three or four days on the job were spent being introduced to coworkers, sitting in a few meetings in which I was listening and some discussions about my first impressions with Mr. Kucha. I outlined my first impressions to Mr. Kucha as follows:

1. Very well prepared and competent R&D engineers that gave me open and honest information, although the leader is weak.
2. Production engineers, with several exceptions, weak and ineffective. The directors of production departments honest but had no confidence in their leader VP of manufacturing.
3. The senior director of product assurance admitted that the quality of the products was not adequate, but he was powerless to stop shipment of poor quality products to customers.
4. There was no strong and independent product testing department.
5. The product and production overhead cost accounting was strange to say the least and I had difficulty understanding it. For example: what did it mean "earned scrap"? To me scrap was a loss; later I established that our product cost accounting was erroneous in some cases.
6. Sales and marketing departments were unhappy with the product quality and unreliable product deliveries.

One incident that stays in my mind was the comment of the VP of manufacturing during our interview. I asked him for an explanation when I noticed a pile of finished and unfinished products with defective tags, which in some cases were older than 30 days. His answer was: "This is the *bone pile* of defective machines; we will fix them when we have time".

I expressed my doubts about the ability to fix these defective machines and told Mr. Kucha that in my opinion this so-called "bone pile" would never be fixed and would have to be written off as scrap, which in fact is what happened.

My first impressions signaled to me what to expect in the coming months. From some of my managers I did not expect reliable advice. It was even worse when during one meeting I asked several department managers what percentage of returned defective products was acceptable. The answers were between 5 and 8%. Later I found out that the return rate of defective products was closer to 15%. These erroneous opinions came from development and manufacturing engineers and some production managers.

During the discussion they asked me about my expectations regarding defective product returns. I told them that during the coming year we would have to improve product quality to such a level where defective product returns from the field would be less than one percent annualized. In many faces I could see smiles and disbelief. I told them in no uncertain terms that we would reach this product quality level with them or with a new management team. At that point, in my mind, I decided that for a period of time I would have to act independently and sometimes dictatorially and would have to make some changes in the management team.

The other surprising news was that no one could tell me the timeframe for the production cycle in the factory for any given product; the guesses were from a week to four weeks. After considerable effort I was told that the product manufacturing cycle time was 37 days. What was worse, some of the production managers and manufacturing engineers did not know why the product manufacturing cycle was important. I calmly explained that parts taking more than a month to convert into finished products were detrimental in two ways:

1. The money sitting in inventory did not bring profits until the customer received the product and paid for it.

2. The product quality improvements could not be implemented until the old parts were in the product manufacturing cycle.

Another situation that was new to Iomega was an "open door" policy. Open door meant that every employee had the right to appeal, which was to come to me if she/he did not receive satisfactory resolution of their problems from their managers, following the chain of command of the organization. This rule caused consternation with my managers for they feared that I would side with the workers and thus undermine their authority. In reality it was the opposite; I was very careful deciding how to solve a possible misunderstanding between workers and their supervisors. Most of the time, the complainants (plaintiffs) wanted me to listen to their stories and asked for no changes in their supervisors' rulings. Sometimes, there were complex issues, but those were in the minority. Sometimes the workers came to me with strictly personal problems not wishing to reveal personal or family problems to their immediate supervisors. This order of mine had positive results: managers began to pay attention to the worker's affairs and work conditions.

My first and very difficult decision was to stop shipment of substandard quality products to customers. I decided that the product quality had to improve by at least 50% before resumption of shipments. Out of my subordinates only the senior director of quality, Travis Smith, agreed enthusiastically with my decision. The other subordinates, in my opinion, agreed with my decision reluctantly, because they had no other choice unless they wanted to resign. The whole production, product development and manufacturing engineering staffs were directed to a product quality improvement program; all other activities stopped. I outlined my decision to the sales, marketing, finance and human resources departments asking for their support and assistance in the product quality improvement program. I created a special product improvement task force from operations, finance and sales and marketing representatives and gave them a lot of freedom in decision-making. I requested that the progress be measured by days, weeks and months. I stated that we had three months to reach satisfactory quality results and only then would we be able to ship all products to our customers. Under certain circumstances we would be shipping products before reaching the 50% quality improvement goals, but that had to meet my approval.

At the same time I found a determined and bright engineer of Polish decent, Peter Kleczkowski, whom I appointed as director of the product testing department with wide authority and responsibility. I continued with further departmental reorganization. I released the vice president of manufacturing, assigned the product testing department to the quality assurance organization, released the manufacturing engineering director and one manager, demanded from the manufacturing directors stronger leadership and gave them more authority and accountability. At the beginning of December I released the vice president of R&D. As expected, I received praises and criticisms from my coworkers.

After maybe two months, Mr. Kucha, the acting president, called me into his office and wondered if I could be more gentle with subordinates and create a more participative rather than dictatorial environment in the operations organization. I explained to him that my personality is to work harmoniously with all coworkers. I did not want to be a dictator and I hated myself every morning. However, considering Iomega's situation, having weak or inexperienced managers in some departments, I did not see any other way other than to take the whole responsibility on myself for maybe six months and try to save the company from possible demise. He agreed with my reasoning and promised to defend me and support me in case of complaints from my subordinates. Later I found out that indeed many times he defended me and justified my actions to my subordinates who lodged complaints against me. My administrative assistant, Dolores Valdez, was completely trustworthy, supportive and in the difficult hours offered encouraging words and help. Occasionally she was asked how she could work for such a tyrant—that is, me. I do not know what her answers were, but judging from coworkers' attitude, they must have been positive.

Although I was hurt hearing the disparaging remarks about me, the outlined work was going forward. In about four months we achieved planned quality improvements and in December we began to ship quality products to our customers. At the end of November, the board chairman asked me how long it would take to achieve desired quality and manufacturing cost improvements. I told him that it would take about five or six months of hard work. He was somewhat dubious if we could reach such results but I assured him that we would make our planned targets.

I remember well, after exactly five months, the chairman called me over the phone and asked if we achieved our stated goals. I told him that many of our objectives are met and reminded him that we still had another month to go. He laughed and said that he would check with me in a month. He clearly knew our progress from the monthly and verbal reports, but surely wanted to remind me that he had not forgotten my promises.

At the end of 1987 we could take pride in the achieved results (Figures taken from the 1987 Annual Report). Raw material, work in process, and finished goods were 18% of yearly revenue compared to 30% at the end of 1986. The last quarter of 1987 had about two-and-a-half-million dollars profit compared to the previous nine-month losses. Product quality improved about 50% compared to the previous year. Manufacturing product cost decreased over 30%; at this point we were selling products at a profit.

On a personal note, because of the demand of work, during New Year's Eve I stayed in Utah while Fran was in Pennsylvania. I celebrated the New Year at Peter Kleczkowski's house with some coworkers and at the stroke of midnight in Pennsylvania we called Fran. She was greeted by what appeared to be a rowdy crowd and, of course, she did not know any of the people that were talking to her, so one can imagine what was going through her mind. Later on she was told that it was a joke. I am not sure how she took the greeting, but judging by the future, everything turned out OK.

### *Goals Met; Costs Reduced!*

In March of 1988 I could tell that we would reach our planned objectives. I suggested that Fran to come to Utah to visit me and maybe start looking for a place to live. During her visit we found a piece of land and entered into a contract to build a house. After long and sometimes acrimonious misunderstandings, on October 24 we finally moved into our house in Ogden, Utah.

By May of 1988 we achieved not only our planned product quality improvements, but most importantly, our product manufacturing costs were better than planned. In the product cost summaries I eliminated that silly expression "earned scrap" and pounded into coworkers heads that scrap is NOT EARNED, but in fact it is an added product cost, that needed to be minimized to zero.

Now we were able to sell our product at a profit. The next major project was to minimize raw material, work in progress and finished goods inventory by more than 60%. This improvement was important in several respects. For starters, the reduction in inventory allowed us to make faster quality and cost reduction improvements. Smaller inventory freed money for other uses, such as new product development and or sales and marketing expansion.

In January of 1988 Iomega created a new division, BOSCO (Bernoulli Optical Systems Company) to exploit optical data storage technology. The division was the result of our entering into an optical technology development agreement with the British Imperial Chemical Industries (ICI). The responsibility of this division was assigned to me; therefore I added a title as president of BOS-CO. The headquarters of this division was Boulder, Colorado. I traveled to Boulder about once a month to meet with the engineers and ICI visitors.

During the first six months of 1988 I found the vice president for R&D, director of manufacturing engineering and several high caliber engineers, also promoted several outstanding engineers and managers. From the finance department, I convinced John Thompson, an outstanding individual, to join operations as materials and logistics vice president. His department had the responsibility for materials control, procurement, transportation and manufacturing engineering services. I gained confidence in the new team and in their work and advice. The positive results gave me an opportunity to loosen the tight grip on my associates and I began building participative team spirit, which I longed to do for almost a year. There was some skepticism about my intentions in participative management approach including disbelief that I would give more authority to my subordinates and carry it out, however, my openness and example convinced my team albeit slowly.

It took about six to nine months before everybody believed in my intentions and behavior. It was my great pleasure to see the progress at work, gaining coworkers' trust and having a team that worked in unison for the good of all members.

The year 1988 was much better than the previous year. At the end of the year it was a pleasure to note achieved results (Results taken from the 1998 Annual Report):

1. Finished goods and raw materials inventory at the end of the year was 15% of annual revenue compared to 18% the end of 1987. It is worth noting that the total revenue for 1988 was over $111 million compared to about $89 million for 1987.
2. Profit for the year was over eight-and-a-half-million dollars compared to an almost thirty-seven-million-dollar loss in 1987. The 1988 results were achieved with improved manufacturing costs and lower overhead costs.
3. Product quality improved about 40% compared to 1987.
4. Product manufacturing costs were lower by about 30% compared to 1987.

The company had a great Christmas party and it was a joy to meet the workers and their spouses in the greatly deserved celebration. Personally, I was satisfied with the leadership of Mr. Kucha, with the chairman of the board, Mr. Dunn and other members of the board, but most importantly I was delighted to have a great team. In October, Fran and I moved into our new house in South Ogden, Utah. I was making a reasonably good living and waited with anticipation of even better success in the coming year.

I was satisfied with the work and achievements during 1988, although in the later part of the year I endured sad news. On November 7 I received a letter from Lithuania that on October 28 my father died; that day was his 88th birthday. At that time Lithuania was still under Soviet rule and it was impossible to notify me in a timely manner. Even if I had known, I am certain that I would not have been given a visa to attend my father's funeral. I knew of several similar situations and in each case visas were not granted to enter the Soviet Union for funerals.

## *TQC and CFM*

At the beginning of 1989, Mr. Kucha, who was tired of traveling every weekend from Utah to his family in California, began a search for a new president and CEO for Iomega. There were three candidates that were interviewed by our executive team. After the interviews we unanimously concluded that the best candidate was Mr. Fred Wenninger. The chairman of the board and certainly the other members of the board entered into an agreement with Mr. Wenninger, who in May started as Iomega's new president. He was highly educated, had a Ph.D. in engineering, possessed exceptional abilities in grasping the issues at hand and had a very pleasant personality. I had the privilege to work closely with him and quickly gained his trust in me.

One day, shortly after he started working at Iomega, he asked me if I knew the Total Quality Control (TQC). I told him that I had heard about it and wondered if it was similar or the same as the Total Quality Management, although I did not have a chance to work with this technology for quality improvements. He gave me a one-hour dissertation about TQC and at the end of the conversation he asked me what I thought about it. I told him very quickly that we indeed needed TQC, because what we achieved up to the present was strictly through intuition, common sense and sweat. I also asked him how we could get somebody with TQC knowledge to help us. He gave me several consultants' names and telephone numbers, suggesting that I get in touch with them directly.

I succeeded in convincing my associates that we needed TQC in all our endeavors and shortly thereafter we began to work with several consultants. After about six months we achieved extraordinary results in product cost, quality and shortened product manufacturing cycle time. We also substantially reduced finished goods and raw material inventory and about a year later we began to see improvements in product development time.

After achieving such improvements, Mr. Wenninger told me that when he gave me a dissertation on TQC, he was not sure if I really believed in it or agreed to it so fast just to please him. He said that his doubts disappeared after seeing how fast I convinced my coworkers and proceeded to work with the consultants without his urging.

We used TQC in all our work; in product development, manufacturing engineering, logistics, production, and even in our paperwork. We showed our results to our suppliers and suggested that they also embrace TQC. Some used our suggestions and were thankful for the improvements, which were also beneficial to us due to better quality and reduced cost from those suppliers. The TQC practices were also implemented in other departments although at a considerably slower pace. I was convinced that the other department heads such as finance and sales and marketing did not think that TQC was applicable in their operations. However, the success in operations eventually convinced them to accept TQC in their departments.

Another innovation, Continuous Flow Manufacturing (CFM), was successfully implemented in our manufacturing processes which shortened product manufacturing cycle time and best of all, substantially reduced work in process.

Our outstanding results using TQC spread to local and more distant businesses and universities—including invitations to give seminars. In these seminars I received considerable assistance from my sr. director of quality, Mr. Travis Smith, and TQC instructor, Ms. Sharon Sarlo. They also received invitations to present papers on TQC. I encouraged them to do as much as was possible, because this was a good advertisement for our company. In the subsequent couple years I received more than ten invitations to give talks on TQC, which I accepted with pleasure.

The year 1989 was considerably better than 1988. At the end of the year we had achieved the following results (Figures taken from the 1989 Annual Report):

1. Finished goods, raw material and work in process at the end of the year was 9.5% of annualized revenue compared to 15% for 1988.

2. Profits reached over 11 million dollars, considering that the R&D expenses were increased by 10% compared to the previous year.

3. Product quality improved by about 30% compared to 1988.

4. Product manufacturing cost was reduced by 35% compared to the previous year.

We had a beautiful Christmas party for the workers and their spouses. The workers morale was exceptionally high; all were satisfied with the achievements and their superiors. The new president and his wife presented themselves to the workers with grace and style. I also was very satisfied with the comments from the workers to my wife saying that they would like to see me with Iomega for a long time. I promised them, that allowing my health, I would remain an Iomega employee until retirement or as long as my superiors would keep me as operations vice president.

# Chapter X

## Trips Home and a New Decade

In 1989, a Lithuanian businessman in Chicago organized an excursion to Lithuania. It had been 17 years from my last visit to Lithuania and I longed to see my relatives, visit my old home where I grew up and introduce Fran to my relatives. We ordered the tickets, paid other expenses associated with the trip and about the middle of June we left the United States for Lithuania.

Although Lithuania was still part of the Soviet Union, the political "straight jacket" that I discovered in 1972, was now considerably relaxed. For example; we could travel for a few days to our former homes, local people freely criticized the

Soviet-Communist government, there were several newspapers printed without censorship, and the Lithuanian flag was displayed in government buildings. This was close to freedom, because the Lithuanian flag was prohibited in 1940 during the first Soviet occupation and the prohibition continued during the second occupation from 1945 till 1990.

From the business point of view the Soviet system was still in force. This meant that the store shelves were virtually empty or had useless products, such as wristwatch bands and clothing buttons. There were better products available in the "hard currency" (Western European, United States, Canadian and Australian currencies) stores. In restaurants one could purchase Perrier water and Western alcoholic drinks only with foreign currency, of which local people had very little or none at all. If I remember, the old law governing foreign currency was still in force, which meant that if local people had foreign currency, they were breaking the law. Alas, in those days many laws were being broken, but the government bureaucrats seeing that the Communist system was falling apart, looked the other way.

In restaurants the food choices, preparation and service were still based on the Soviet order, which meant that no matter how many different meals were on the menu, one could only get maybe two or three, poor quality, offerings. One huge difference compared with 1972 was the faces of the people. In the streets one could see many smiling faces. Local people were anxious to talk to foreigners, especially Americans. Some were offering currency exchanges at black market rates that were two or three times better than the official rate of exchange.

Meeting my relatives was with tears, hugs and smiles. How wonderful it was to see my mother, introduce Fran, her daughter-in-law, and only briefly discuss the past. Regretfully, my father was no longer there, but all the other relatives came to my mother's house. It was wonderful to see smiling faces, hear criticism of the Communist government and hope for a better future. The independence of Lithuania was freely discussed and it was not if but when.

The principal of Plutiškės middle school invited me to give a brief description about the differences between Lithuanians living in the United States and those living in Lithuania.

As a side note, I would like to remind the readers that my first four years of schooling was in Plutiškės, although at that time there were only four grades which was the mandatory educational level.

Regrettably, I do not have the notes, but as much as I remember I told the students that Lithuanians living anywhere in the world love their country of origin and cherish the memories. The difference between us living in the United States and those living in Lithuania is in the morning, when we wake up we seen the American sky while you see the Lithuanian sky. I explained to the students that we long to visit Lithuania and hope for a better future to our country of origin. I urged them to study hard, love their country and work towards the good of all Lithuanian people.

We visited many of my relatives not only in the vicinity of Plutiškės but also in Kaunas and Vilnius. All the relatives were very gracious hosts with mountains of food wherever we went. Both Fran and I still talk about how many meals we had to have each day. All wanted to spend more time with us and were full of questions about our life in United States. It is with great regret that after two weeks we had to go back home.

With sorrow I met my Aunt Marija, Uncle Klemensas Gustaitis' wife. She was living with my Cousin Leon Gustaitis. When we went there, we were met with great fanfare and Lithuanian-style hospitality, which in my judgment is the most gracious and generous of any people. We spent the night there. I noted that my aunt sometimes could not remember me; my mother had to prompt her as to my identity. During her wedding I fell in love with this new, elegant aunt. My mother explained to me that my Aunt Marija had lost part of her memory, which was confirmed to me by Cousins Leon and Klemensas Gustaitis and Janina Kačergienė (nee Gustaitytė). I was not surprised with that, considering what she had to endure during Stalin's Communist rule. Their family was deported to Siberia, I believe in 1947, where for 12 years they endured inhuman conditions. My Cousin Janina was only one-and-a-half days old when they were herded into cattle cars without food and drinking water for more than a week.

From the discussions with my mother and my cousins, I learned that Aunt Marija had to live alone with the children for several years before Uncle Klemensas was permitted to join them. Any wonder that she lost some of her mind. This was not an isolated incident; thousands of Lithuanians, Latvians and Estonians endured a similar fate.

One interesting and humorous incident occurred while we were at my Cousin Leon's house. Fran and my sleeping quarters were on the second floor. A half-bath was on the first floor while the bathtub was in the basement. The next morning Fran wanted to take a bath and asked me to go with her to the basement. While descending downstairs suddenly very strange noises scared Fran half to death. It really was not some kind of ghost but merely young turkey chicks brought in the basement for the night to keep warm. To this day, I sometimes tease her about her fear of the turkey chicks at my cousin's house.

After two weeks we left Lithuania and having spent one night in Moscow flew back to the United States. We brought back many wonderful memories and gifts from the relatives. We invited some of our friends over and shared our experiences, while at work I had to tell my coworkers what I experienced and saw in my native land.

### European Operations

The practice of TQC and CFM continued in the New Year at Iomega. The achieved results gave us increased profits and improved the confidence of our customers and suppliers. The product quality improved so much that we were able to extend our new product warranty from one to five years. The five year warranty was unprecedented in our industry.

Our product sales were going better than in 1989. New product introductions helped, although better marketing plans compared with previous years was also a factor in improved sales. The only geographical area that did not achieve satisfactory results was Europe. Our sales offices in Belgium and Germany and sales/distribution agents in other Western European countries did not meet the planned sales objectives. I traveled in all major European distribution and sales locations trying to understand what caused the deficiencies in our plans.

In Belgium we had our European sales and marketing headquarters. After spending several days there I came to the conclusion that our European vice president, who was an American, was too enamored with the elegant European lifestyle, evening dinners and sumptuous parties, and spent too much time in these pleasures, rather than paying strong attention and discipline to sales. He also had only a few satisfactory subordinates. I tried to explain to him that business is like a war, and in war as in business, there is no substitute for victory. I pointed out to him that he had to understand his strengths and limitations, his competition and his customers. I was under the impression that he treated these business truisms superficially.

While traveling to other European countries I noticed that the German country manager was diligent and demanded a high level of commitment and fulfillment of sales plans from his subordinates. Sometimes he even traveled and encouraged our Italian sales agents for he spoke Italian fluently.

Spain left me a curious impression. For example, work officially starts at eight or nine o'clock in the morning, however the workers come in between eight and ten a.m. A meeting time is set at a designated hour but it may start on time or an hour later and no one pays any attention. Lunch starts around one p.m. and ends about four p.m. After a well prepared, abundant meal and ample wine, work continues lasting until eight p.m.—in my opinion, cannot be carried out with diligence. Dinner starts around nine or ten p.m. and lasts three or four hours. I was astonished that in spite of the unusual, at least to Americans, living customs and behavior, Spaniards were able to sell our products in accordance with the established plans.

Recently I heard that Spaniards, since joining the European Union, are carrying out their work and living habits similarly to the other European countries and the habits of the United States. This change has happened at least to those that work, while the older people and non-working aristocrats probably live by the old standards.

### Home without a Visa

One more incident worth mentioning was Iomega's wish to display and demonstrate our products at a technical show in Moscow which took place in March, 1990. Because I could speak Russian and knew Russian culture, I decided to visit the show. I received a visa to Moscow without difficulty, but the Soviet government refused me a visa to Lithuania. I told Fran that I wanted to visit relatives in Lithuania, but did not tell her that I did not have a visa to go there. She prepared two large suitcases of various products including 30 pair of pantyhose. To fix the impression of the show I purchased a camcorder.

When I came to Shermetejevo airport, which was for foreign travel only, I noticed a very "dedicated" group of customs agents. They opened every suitcase, took out all the belongings and inspected everything in detail. What to do with 30 pair of pantyhose?! Shortly before handing my documents to the customs agent I lit up a cigarette and offered one to the agent. He took the cigarette and noticing the camcorder on my shoulder, wanting to know what it was. I cheerfully explained to him what it was and recorded a short strip and showed him how he looked at his work. He asked me how much the camcorder cost and could it be connected to a Soviet television. I explained to him that the Soviet television system is different from the American system therefore this camcorder would not work on a Soviet TV. Our discussion lasted maybe 15 minutes. In the meantime I lit up another cigarette and offered one to him. I also told him that I had enough cigarettes and offered him a full pack, which he took quickly. In the meantime our line was getting longer and I noticed many unhappy faces. Finally I showed him my three suitcases and politely asked which one he would like to see first. He just waved his hand, stamped the declaration form and told me to proceed. After thanking him warmly I walked to the taxi line.

I took a taxi to Vnukovo airport which, at that time, was used for internal air transport only. Because I already had a ticket from Moscow to Vilnius, which I purchased in the United States, I got onto the plane and in a couple of hours I was met at Vilnius airport by my relatives. I spent a couple of pleasant days with my relatives and with a laugh told them the story about my encounter with the customs agent in Shermetejevo airport. We talked a lot about the political situation in Lithuania, because at that time Lithuania was demanding independence and separation from the Soviet Union. The situation was very tense because in that February's elections almost all non-communists were elected in the country's Soviet parliament. I received indirect information that the newly elected Lithuanian parliament would declare independence on March 11. On the 10th of March, with a heavy heart, I left Lithuania for Moscow.

Indeed, on the 11th of March 1990, the Lith-

uanian parliament declared the country's independence. In the following year the Lithuanian people
experienced many difficulties and shortages in
supplies such as oil that came from other Soviet
republics. There were also threats and the spilling
of blood near the Vilnius television transmission
tower, all for wanting independence from the Soviet Union. Finally, under pressure from the United States and other Western European countries,
Gorbachev, sitting on a collapsing Soviet imperial
chair, at the beginning of September 1991, was
forced to acknowledge Lithuanian independence.
In a few days the independent Lithuania was accepted as a member of the United Nations.

During registration at the Rossiya Hotel in
Moscow the clerk asked me where I was for the
prior four days. I told her that I visited my relatives
in Lithuania. Then she wanted to know what hotel I stayed at in Lithuania. I told her that I stayed
with my relatives. Then she inquired whether I
registered in the local police station. I answered
that having conversations with many relatives I
completely forgot to register in the police station
as required by law. In reality, I could not have registered because I did not have a visa for Lithuania.
The lady clerk told me that I would have to pay a
fine. Without objections I agreed and the "fine"
cost me $1.65. After getting a receipt for the "fine"

in triplicate I politely thanked her and went to my designated room.

When I tried to take a taxi from the hotel to the exhibition hall, the taxi drivers wanted dollars not rubles. After agreeing on the price in dollars, I traveled to the exhibition which was housed in the Communist Achievement Palace. What was interesting, the taxi driver was criticizing the Soviet system saying that Americans, being very rich, can afford to send astronauts to space, but the Soviet government has no business sending cosmonauts to space while ordinary people cannot buy a pair of shoes. While driving by the Derzhinski statue near Liubiyanka prison, he laughingly commented that the current rulers of that place (meaning KGB) have nowhere near the power that their predecessor had. From such and other conversations with Russians I formed an opinion that the people in the Soviet Union were not happy with the regime and freely expressed their feelings. At the time of Stalin and even some time later, such expressions would have earned them 25 years in a Siberian slave labor camp.

The exhibits showed no new, unseen before products, because many American and Western European products were shown earlier in various exhibits in Europe and the United States. The difference was that most Russians had not seen such technological marvels and the visitor numbers would be the envy of any show in the Western world.

As it was the custom then in the Soviet Union, foreign exhibit participants had separate kitchens and dining halls. Of course, all the services and food was paid in advance with dollars. The food preparation was excellent, maybe even outlandish. My cousins' son, Giedrius Vegys, came to the exhibit as my guest, and after seeing various products including Iomega products we had an opportunity to have a meal in this enclave reserved for foreigners.

From the service people I had offers to buy caviar at prices substantially lower than in the United States. I offered a somewhat lower price and the server agreed to sell it to me for one-fourth of the US price. I brought home enough cans of caviar sufficient not only for me but also as gifts. When I asked the server where he got the caviar he, with a smile, told me that it was "organized," in other words, stolen. It was the same thing with alcoholic drinks in bottles not only in the exhibition hall but in the hotel's dining rooms as well.

The service in the hotel, bed sheets and towels were of Soviet quality. My room service, bed sheets and towel quality improved markedly when I gave gifts of nylon stockings and chocolate to my floor supervisor.

After returning home, I had to give a trip summary to my associates and Iomega executives and show the tape that I made with my camcorder. I also confessed to Fran about the fact that I went to Lithuania without a visa and had I been caught, I most likely would have been arrested. Fran gave me a reprimand that was much sterner and considerably longer than the one given by the hotel clerk in Moscow.

In the late summer of 1990, Iomega arranged a European sales agents meeting in Rome. It was interesting to meet the European sales agents and Iomega's own European sales people. I had an opportunity to listen to their performance reports and plans for the coming year. During the evening social hour I was able to tell them what was going on in the world headquarters in Roy, Utah. Fran and I had an opportunity to spend some time alone and do sightseeing in Rome. Although this was not our first time in Rome, the eternal city is always fascinating no matter how many times one visits it. We spent over a week in Italy and came back to America prepared for new challenges at work.

## Starting the New Decade

At the beginning of 1990 we entered into a licensing agreement with Insite Peripherals Co. for its Floptical technology, which provides high density read and write capability on the standard 3-1/2 inch floppy disks. By using special Floptical media containing optical grooves, the capacity is increased to 20 megabytes from 1.44 megabytes in a single floppy size cartridge. The development of this product was assigned to the BOSCO division in Colorado which reported to me. Insite Peripherals was located in California and the BOSCO division in Colorado, therefore I had to travel at least once a month to those locations to finalize various licensing agreements. The development expenses for the Floptical product was high in comparison with the R&D expenses in Utah, while sales for this product was not expected for the next two years.

In February 1990, in San Diego, California we started a new division for a Magnetic Tape Drive development. This product, when developed, would be used as a backup device for the increasing hard disk capacity of the PC. The president of this new division was reporting to the Iomega president, hence I did not have to worry about this new division. The financial picture, about which I was concerned, was such that although the development costs were incurred at the start, the revenue was not anticipated for the following two years. I had conversations with our chief financial officer regarding our new product development expenses, wondering if we were not overreaching—he agreed with me.

I expressed my concerns regarding the high R&D expenses to our president, but he assured me that our sales and marketing vice president had plans to increase revenue and profits for the current products that year. Indeed, our revenue increased over 10% compared to the prior year, but R&D expenses increased by almost 18% over the prior year.

Since the revenue, profits and product quality increased, the company was able to pay bonuses to all workers, which were distributed twice a year; in August for the first six months and January for the last six months of the year.

At the end of the year the results were as follows (Figures taken from 1990 Annual Report):

1. The inventory (raw materials, finished goods and work in process) at the end of the year was 8% of annualized revenue compared to 9.5% at the end of 1989. It is important to note that 80% of the inventory was in raw material therefore we were able to implement quality improvements and cost reductions faster.

2. Profits reached over $14 million compared with a little over $11 million the previous year, even when R&D and sales and marketing expenses increased over $7 million compared to 1989.

3   The product manufacturing cost decreased about 11% compared to 1989.

4.  Product quality increased about 32% compared to the prior year.

Although our product sales were satisfactory in the United States and Canada, the European contribution was less than expected. In order to increase European sales we decided, amongst other things, to transfer some production from the United States to Europe. My boss, the president, asked me to find suitable facilities in Western Europe. I invited Peter Kleczkowski to help me. Because we both were born and grew up in Europe, we had a somewhat better understanding about European production opportunities. We spent several weeks in various European countries and decided that the best manufacturing opportunities existed in Belgium and Holland. Although Germany was our largest European market, the working conditions were much more restrictive than Holland, and the corporate income taxes in Germany were the highest in Western Europe.

The newly appointed European operations vice president ignored our search and suggestions. He decided to locate the European headquarters in Germany. At that time I thought that he knew Germany better than I did for he spent a number of years with Hewlett Packard in Germany. His choice of location however was questionable. He chose the vicinity of Freiburg, which is a university town located in the southwest corner of Germany, near the Swiss and French borders. There were no high technology industries nearby and air transport to and from United States was terrible; one had to go either to the Frankfurt airport and then travel over 100 miles and change to a train or go to Zurich, Switzerland and again make a change in trains. Of course, the beauty of the Black Forest and reasonably agreeable climate made life and leisure quite pleasant. I could not fault him on that.

I was very satisfied with our accomplishments, but in my opinion, we had one gathering dark cloud and that was the rate our expenses were increasing compared with revenue and profit increases.

In general, the year 1990 was good to me not only professionally but personally as well. All our family, including my children, were healthy. David graduated from the university in the spring of 1991 and was planning get a job in Iomega—during the prior couple summers while working in Iomega, he received high praises from his superiors.

### The Year 1991

Because the year 1990 was the best in Io-mega's history, with high hopes and expectations we started 1991. In all departments we practiced TQC and CFM which allowed us to further improve quality and efficiency in all phases of our business.

In January we purchased a new thin film technology including patents, documents, equipment and material inventory from Springer Technologies Co. We anticipated this technology to be used in our new, not yet developed products, and improvements in the existing products. We did not expect to derive any benefits including profits from this technology for the next two years. We left the division headquarters in the old Springer Technologies location in Fremont, CA and canceled the Springer Technology name. The new technology research and ultimately product development was assigned to me. Understanding how much work would be required in the new division I asked and was granted to relinquish my duty as president of BOSCO. That job was assigned to one of my colleges, Sr. Vice President Anton Radman.

During the year we saw a need to incorporate some software in our products and create subsystems which could be plugged directly into a PC. That way the customer would not have to worry about finding technical consultants that would incorporate our product into their systems for a price. I was assigned the responsibility for

193

this subsystems department. Because I created a cadre of high caliber managers and I trusted them implicitly to carry out their responsibilities, it was easy for me to take on more responsibilities within the Iomega headquarters.

With the increased responsibilities within operations I began to get more involved in our future planning. I had to spend more time with my superior, the president of Iomega. The meetings were always very productive to me because Mr. Wenninger was so easy to work with and for. Sometimes, I would express my concerns about our higher than planned revenue percentage for R&D expenses since we were not meeting our planned monthly revenue and profit targets. My superior would reassure me that the sales and marketing vice president promised to meet the sales targets in the coming months.

After stating my opinion I would continue to do my job. There was one major disagreement with my president involving the purchase of the land and building our European headquarters near Freiburg, Germany. As I mentioned earlier in the book, I agreed very reluctantly to locate our European headquarters in Freiburg.

Regarding the purchase of the land and building the facility, both our CFO and I felt that there was no need to spend the money for land and facilities when there were rentals available at more reasonable prices and without the long term burden of real estate ownership. The CFO and I felt strongly enough about this issue, therefore our president was obligated to notify the board of directors about our objections. The plans for the land and building purchase were terminated and our European headquarters were left in a leased facility in Freiburg. The president and I reconciled our differences, but I felt that the European operations vice president never forgave me for my objections. I did not pay any attention to his feelings; I was concerned about the company's future success in Europe rather than accommodating to the personal desires of a vice president.

In general, Iomega made very good progress during 1991 (Figures are from 1990 Annual Report):

1. At the end of the year the warehouse inventory was 9% of annualized revenue compared to 8% in 1990. The increase in inventory was due to production of new products prior to shipment to distribution and customers.

2. Net income was over $12 million compared to about $14 million in 1990. It must be recognized that in 1991 about $11 million more than in 1990 was spent on increased expenses in R&D, sales and marketing and increases in

Federal income taxes.

3. Product quality increased 15% compared to the previous year. This year we reached the target of 1% annualized product returns due to quality problems. This was the target that I set in 1987.

4. Product cost decreased 3% compared to 1990.

5. Revenue increased over 13% compared to 1990. The European revenue remained about the same as in 1990.

I was satisfied with the overall progress in 1991 except with the development of the thin film technology. The raw materials, as part of the purchase from Springer Technologies, turned out to be worthless. It took the engineers and the director of the division about six months to determine the worthlessness of the raw material. In my opinion that was a very valuable determination and I gave praises to the engineering team and their leader. It was a difficult road ahead to find suitable material for this technology.

In March, my wife and I visited Hanover Fair in Germany where Iomega had a booth and displayed and demonstrated its products. Hanover Fair is the largest technical exhibit in Europe. It is larger and broader than any fair in the United States. Considering the location of Hanover, Fran and I decided to take a couple days vacation and visit united Berlin. While visiting the Berlin wall, Fran chiseled out pieces of the wall, which we have displayed under glass in our house. She also brought some wall pieces as gifts to our friends and relatives.

During the year, while traveling to Europe on business, I had opportunities to visit my mother and other relatives in Lithuania. One time I purchased a box of bananas in Poland and brought them to my relatives whose children had never tasted bananas. Also I brought my mother a bottle of French cognac, which she loved so much and asked me to bring her whenever I came to visit. It was such a small request considering the heartaches she had experienced through the years on my account.

The end of the year passed delightfully with our friends celebrating the New Year in a Salt Lake City hotel and waiting for the next year with anticipation.

# $\mathcal{C}$hapter XI

## 1991 to 1995

As I mentioned earlier, the March 1990 Lithuanian declaration of independence and secession from the Soviet Union conflicted with Gorbachev's plans to continue maintaining the Soviet "Evil Empire" (term coined by former US President Reagan) in one piece. Gorbachev created all sorts of difficulties for the Lithuanian Republic, such as stopping supplies of natural gas and oil and making threats to the legally elected parliamentarians. During his visit to Lithuania he tried to instill fear in the people and finally, on January 13, 1991 issued an order to the Special Forces "Spetznac" to take over the Vilnius television transmission station.

Spetznac, the punitive battalion, well armed with automatic weapons and tanks were advancing towards the TV transmission station. Civilians, without weapons, tried to stop advancing tanks. The results could have been foretold: weaponless civilians lost: thirteen people lost their lives, scores were wounded and the punitive battalion occupied the TV transmission station. Lithuanians immediately began transmissions from Kaunas telling the world what was going on in Vilnius.

When in the spring of 1991 I had an opportunity to visit Lithuania, my cousin's son, Adrijus Vegys, gave me a tour around the parliament building which was surrounded by a barbed wire not only on the ground but on the roof as well. The barbed wire on the roof minimized the possibility of paratrooper landings. He also showed me the place where the thirteen people died while defending the TV transmission station. The story and pictures are fixed on magnetic tape that was prepared by A. Vegys. I am grateful for his efforts, because this is a historical fact which I intend to translate into English and distribute to my children and grand-children, so they will remember what price Lithuanians paid for their freedom from the Soviet Union.

I would like to state once more how happy I was when President Bush and the Western European leaders forced Gorbachev to sign a document at the beginning of September, releasing Lithuania, Latvia and Estonia from the Soviet Union. After a few days all three nations became members of the United Nations.

As it is known in history, on December 25, 1991 Gorbachev signed a document dissolving the Soviet Union, so ended the last empire of the twentieth century—in my opinion, Lithuania contributed substantially to its demise.

## *The Year 1992*

The New Year started reasonably well. For the first three months sales in the United States met the plan, although in Europe, especially in Germany, and to the US Federal Government sales were substantially below plan. TQC and CFM provided improvements, albeit they were smaller than in the past, because we reached 68% of the asymptotic curve where progress is measured in small increments.

In October of 1991 we had a strategic planning meeting in Laguna Niguel, California. The 1992 plan called for over $150 million in sales and over $17 million in profit. These numbers included sales of a new Bernoulli Drive, the Tape Backup Drive and the 20 megabyte Floptical Disk Drive.

Unfortunately expectations and reality were

quite different. The new products, planned to be available for the market in the spring of 1992, in reality were delayed from six to nine months. That meant that the R&D budgets for those products were higher than planned. The result was that the expenses were higher than planned while sales and profits were lower than expected. The actual sales and profits for 1992 were 30-40% lower than planned.

The other difficulty was with the thin film research. As I mentioned earlier, the material that was purchased together with the thin film technology from Springer Technologies, Inc. was worthless. The engineers were forced to find new materials. Here again, the expenses for the Thin Film project were higher than planned. I had to send my best manufacturing engineering director, George Krieger, from Roy, Utah to Fremont, California, to design and develop a new materials laboratory.

All these adversities required unanticipated expenses while at the same time we knew we would not meet our planned sales and profits. Although in our plans we anticipated substantial investments and high risk that some products might not materialize, however this year we had more than our share of adversities.

1992 sales were higher by only 2% compared to the previous year. The North American sales were higher by about 12% while oversees business increased by about 10% even when German sales had fallen substantially. Sales to the Federal Government decreased by about 31% compared to 1991. Our overhead and sales and marketing expenses increased by about 10% over planned budget, while R&D expenses were higher by 22% compared to the previous year (Figures taken from the 1992 Annual Report).

At the end of 1992 it was decided to reorganize the company along product lines. This meant that each product manager (vice president) would have profit and loss responsibility for that product. All product managers/vice presidents reported to me.

These responsibilities were added to my other duties. At the same time I was promoted to the position of chief operating officer, a new position in our company. The promotion brought in not only more responsibilities but increased demands on my time. I became the president's advisor related to all operations matters. The only part of the company that was not under my jurisdiction was finance, sales and marketing and administration. My first advice to the president was to remove the vice president of sales and marketing for substantially failing to deliver 1992 results. In about a month, that is by the end of January, 1993, the vice president of sales and marketing was removed and temporarily, the president assumed the responsibility for that position.

Because the company failed to meet planned results by a wide margin, the president and all vice presidents including myself took a 5% cut in salary and rescinded a planned bonus. Hence, the year 1992 was probably the most difficult in my career at Iomega.

However, not all was bad during the year. We reached and in some cases exceeded planned cost reductions and quality improvements. We received the Shingo Prize for excellence in manufacturing. The praises were accorded not only to the company but to me as well for excellent leadership. I am not sure that I deserved all that praise because there were many people who contributed to the success of our manufacturing quality—thus ended a half successful or half failed year depending upon one's perspective.

## *The Year 1993*

As mentioned earlier, at the end of 1992 we made many organizational changes, thinking that these changes would help to overcome our current difficulties. We, the management team, did not understand the market conditions. We were too slow in understanding the competition and the world economic situation; relying too much on a manager's advise (which later proved to be wrong), and an assumption that more people and coming new technologies would be the factors in improving our current unenviable situation.

In general, the year 1993 was very difficult for Iomega. The sales of older product declined compared to the previous year. We had to reduce prices on older products to successfully compete in the market place. The reduced prices helped in sales but negatively affected profits. The new products had high manufacturing costs compared to competitive sales prices, which did not help the year's profits. The expenses associated with sales and marketing, especially European expenses, reduced potential profits even more. We were forced to reduce R&D expenses the results of which would be felt in the next year and beyond.

In about the middle of June it was obvious that Iomega would have to make unpleasant changes. The board of directors decided to review our business plans and revise them if necessary. After about two months the board requested the resignation of our president. The board also decided to sell the thin film technology division. I was invited to attend a special board meeting not knowing what that meant. I was offered to temporarily take over leadership of the company as acting chief executive officer until the board could find a new president and CEO. I accepted their offer because I could not see another alternative, especially since I had several differences of opinions over operations with the outgoing president.

The chairman asked me to write a profile of a candidate for the position of Iomega president. When I gave the written profile to the chairman he questioned why the profile did not include the experiences that I had. He also wondered if I wanted to be considered as a candidate for the position of the president. I told the chairman that the candidate should have extensive experience in sales and marketing and should be good with investment bankers and news media, the experiences that were not my strong suit. I also told him that I was quite happy in my present position and was prepared to continue to work for the good of the company. I agreed, while carrying out the duties as temporary chief executive, to reduce expenses.

After reviewing the financial situation and in consultation with my coworkers, I decided that company expenses had to be reduced by about $14 million during the rest of that year. This was perhaps the most difficult decision in my career. I had to terminate three vice presidents, about ten directors and a couple hundred coworkers. Many of the coworkers were friends with whom I had a very good working relationship. We also had to take other steps to save money. When all was said and done, we found ways to save the $14 million without affecting the efficiency and morale of the workers. In the annual report I received congratulations in the chairman's letter to the stockholders.

After the layoffs and terminations, I had to recreate the management team. I moved the Manufacturing Engineering Director, George Krieger, to manage the R&D departments in Roy, Utah. Dave Thompson was appointed director of subsystems engineering, and Brian Paston was promoted to director of manufacturing engineering. At the same time, I appointed Jim Kelly as director of tape drive engineering in San Diego, California. Thus at the beginning of 1994 we had a strong and very competent operations management team without adding any additional personnel. We also abandoned the product line management matrix organization and relied upon the normal functional management approach.

While making these changes I had to give advice to the chairman and other members of the board regarding the selection of the new president. Finally in about the middle of December we found a suitable candidate. He agreed to start working at the beginning of January after I finished the restructuring of the organization. The new president's work was easier for he did not have to worry about the reductions in work force and potential savings in expenses; so ended the difficult year 1993.

## *Personal Sorrows*

On February 12th, when I came to work I found a fax from Lithuania, sent by my cousins' son, Giedrius Vegys, stating that on that date my mother passed away. (There is a time difference of nine hours between Utah and Lithuania.) I immediately started the process to obtain a visa and airline tickets. I also notified my Cousin, Marytė Speitinienė, via telephone that I would be coming on Sunday for my mother's funeral. She arranged for my Cousin Klemensas Gustaitis and his wife to come to Vilnius International Airport to meet me. Fran took me to the airport in Salt Lake City and asked me not to grieve too much.

While traveling through Kaunas, my Cousin Klemensas suggested that I buy flowers and a wreath in Kaunas. It never entered my mind that on a Sunday in February one could not find flowers in the village of Plutiškės. I thanked him for his good advice and purchased the flowers in Kaunas.

I was concerned that my Cousin Marytė would have too many expenses related to the funeral, therefore, despite her objections, I gave her money for the casket and other expenses and I bought two piglets that were slaughtered and prepared for the meal after the funeral. In Lithuania it is a custom to have a meal for relatives and those that participated in the funeral, such as the priest, the singers of the funeral rites, the gravediggers, the kitchen help and the casket carriers.

The day of the funeral was exceptionally cold and the Plutiškės church had no heat. I caught a cold because I did not pack warm clothes suitable for that part of the world in February. I had 50-year-old romantic memories of the beauty of the church, the grounds and fences; the reality was they now appeared to be very dull and poorly maintained. It was clear that during the Communist rule not much was done to maintain the church since the government would not give the material permits needed for church repairs.

The funeral services and meal went quite well. I just had a cold and coughed until my return home. I was overjoyed that I could attend my mothers' funeral.  (I only found out about my father's death seven days after the fact.) The Communist system was such that relatives living outside the Soviet Union were unable to participate on such sorrowful days due to communication delays and difficulties in getting visas.

Fran wanted to know everything about the funeral and other activities. I told her all the details and said that my expenses were several hundred dollars for flowers, a wreath, casket, money to the priest for his services and the purchase of two piglets. She laughed and had difficulty understanding until I explained the purpose of the piglets. Even to this day, we occasionally have a laugh about my expenses for mothers' funeral—including the two piglets. In the United States a simple funeral can cost several thousand dollars.

I came home with sorrow in my heart because of mothers' death, but was satisfied that all arrangements for her funeral were well thought out by my Cousin, Marytė Spietinienė. Life has to go on irrespective of the pain one has for the loss of loved ones.

### The Year 1994

During the first three months of 1994 we made many restructuring changes that were planned in the fall of 1993. We sold the thin film magnetic head development division, stopped development of the Floptical disk program and closed the facility terminating all engineering and support staff. After two months we sold the technology, patents, equipment and materials to a 3M division. We made this decision based on market analysis and customer focus groups input. In the last quarter of the year we wrote off old production machinery and closed several nonproductive sales offices in the United States and Europe.

This year was indeed very interesting for Iomega. Our new president had peculiar views about Iomega's past. Stated succinctly, he verbally swept away everything that was achieved in the past, although he did not have a clear plan for the future. He merely stated that we would have to create a new Iomega.

The "new Iomega" in fact, was not just window dressing. The new president brought in a new sales and marketing team, did a lot of customer focus group meetings, engaged a marketing consulting firm, and in general, spent a lot of money. He also talked about new products, which had to be very different from the current product line.

After a couple of months in his job, the president outlined to me the new machine specifications:

1. 100 megabyte removable magnetic disk storage drive.

2. Outside diameter of the disk cartridge not larger than 3-½ inches.

3. The retail sales price for the drive less than $200, which meant that the manufacturing cost had to be less than $100 for the disk cartridge sales price to be $20.

4. The new product would have to be demonstrated at the COMDEX show in Las Vegas, Nevada in November of 1994.

In summary, this meant that product development, testing and building a number of prototype units had to be accomplished in about nine months. Similar products normally require about two years of engineering work. Most importantly, the manufacturing cost of this new product had to be about half compared to other Iomega and competitive product costs. Although we had similar products in our engineering laboratories, to me the time frame for this program appeared to be too ambitious. I asked the president to give me a few days to think about it and talk to my associates.

When I related our president's wishes and the new product specifics to my associates, they, with the exception of two directors and two vice presidents, had a good laugh and stated that it was a "pipe dream" and insanity. After a few days' discussions and my determination that the program could be implemented, and with the agreement of one vice president and several directors in engineering and production, I advised the president that we were prepared to execute his proposed plan. He thanked me for my efforts and with a smile wished us good luck. Before leaving his office I opined that this new product, without good sales and marketing, would meet the same fate as many excellent products that were in the bone pile of industrial failures. He told me not to worry about it for he had a few good sales and marketing candidates from his previous company.

We began to walk or better stated, to run this difficult short road, immersing ourselves in the development, testing and construction of this new product. The coworkers in engineering and the testing and production departments worked harmoniously and put in many hours of work, even on Saturdays and Sundays. I fully understood their dedication and spent many evenings with these hard working folks. The work continued without major hitches especially when I convinced several directors in engineering and manufacturing to make sure that the departmental walls were abolished and that all work like they were part of one department.

While our work progressed, the president indeed fulfilled his promise to find good people in the sales and marketing departments. He hired about seven high-ranking executives that, at least on the surface, appeared to be knowledgeable and alert. Mentally I decided that I would pass judgment when I saw their sales, advertising and marketing plans. In the meantime, the expenses for sales and marketing were rising like a racket. Sometimes I would talk to the VP of finance and some other coworkers and expressed an opinion regarding the sales and marketing expenses. I thought that perhaps they were spending too much money in preparatory work, including large sums for consultants who gave advice on the outside appearance of the product and advertising in preparation for a show in November. Several of my coworkers and I were astonished at the product name and color; just think, the disk drive name was **Zip** and the color **cobalt blue**! One should remember that until then computer equipment colors were putty gray.

Occasionally we had interdepartmental disagreements, but in general, the work continued smoothly and according to plan. The president announced that he wanted to change Iomega from a technology-driven to a customer-driven company. His favored expression was "give the customer what he wants, when he wants it and a price he is willing to pay". This appeared as a very simple suggestion, although to implement it we needed to change many coworkers' minds and change the company culture. I was of the opinion that we had to make dramatic changes because the earlier approaches of the prior three or four years did not produce acceptable results. I personally tried to help the president by preaching his views to my co-workers which comprised about 80% of the company.

While making strategic changes towards the customers, we did not neglect our achievements in quality. Our products had the highest quality in comparison with other computer equipment products. Although our product quality was the highest, the sales volume was about the same as in the previous couple of years.

The 1994 business statistics were as follows (Figures taken from the 1994 Annual Report):

1.  The revenue was about $142 million compared with $147 in 1993.
2.  Operating expenses, after the end of the 1993 restructuring, were close to $50 million compared to about $70 million the previous year.
3.  The losses were about $2 million compared to over $14 million lost in 1993. Of importance was the fact that the second half of 1994 was profitable.
4.  At the end of 1994 the cash on hand was almost $20 million compared to $19 million the previous year. The cash in 1994 increased only $1 million while marketing and sales expenses were slightly higher in 1994. However, the revenue base in 1994 was lower by about $5 million.

During the month of October we knew that our new product, the ZIP removable disk drive, would be demonstrated at COMDEX at the end of November in Las Vegas, Nevada. Before the COMDEX show our sales and marketing organization, under confidentiality agreements, demonstrated ZIP products to several news media representatives, potential buyers and focus user groups. From the user groups and technical journal reporters we received unbelievable praises. At that point we understood that we had an unusual product.

Internally we questioned ourselves how many units we could sell in 1995. The sales and marketing organization estimates were between 120- and 180-thousand ZIP drives and between 600- and 900-thousand ZIP cartridges.

The 1994 COMDEX show in Las Vegas was unqualified success for our company. During the show the ZIP drive was introduced to an enthusiastic reception from industry analysts, the trade press and potential customers. During the five-day show our booth was overflowing with people: journalists, potential buyers, curious visitors and representatives of our competitors. There was no question about the success of the ZIP product. My personal opinion was that we probably could sell more than 200-thousand Zip drives in 1995, but I was not successful in convincing our sales and marketing organization about such volumes.

My responsibility as chief operating officer was engineering, manufacturing and quality, but not finance. I had to convince the chief financial officer to commit the company to purchase parts for more than 250-thousand units. The CFO and the president agreed with my estimates and I, based on their concurrence, committed the company to a high financial risk, more than $30 million.

Iomega engineers were able to design and produce the ZIP drive for one-third the cost of any similar Iomega product while retaining the required performance characteristics. The ZIP drive was offered to end users for under $200 and 100-megabyte disks for less than $20—a dramatic leapfrog over industry price/performance stan-dards.

Although ZIP products created unparalleled success for the company, we still put a lot of ef-fort into other Iomega products, such as Bernoulli drives with the highest reliability reputation in the industry and Ditto tape drives, the easiest to use product for computer back-up needs.

1994 changed Iomega from a technology driv-en, inwardly focused niche supplier, into a custom-er-driven vendor to the broad personal computer market. We reached new horizons in new markets, new users and new products. The users and clients became the center of whatever we did. With aggressive sales and marketing plans based on market research, our main aim was to give customers what they wanted, when they wanted and at the price they were willing to pay. For me personally the year 1994 demanded a lot of work, nerves and dedication, but the results were worth it; the year was one of the best in my professional career.

## The Year 1995

The year 1995 is one of the more interesting ones I remember in my life. It was unparalleled hard work, high risk and indescribable joy with the results achieved. Herewith are some milestones for the year:

**March 7:** The Ditto family of tape backup products offered the industry's first $99 tape backup drive.

**March 24:** Iomega's innovative Zip drive and disks began shipping to customers in production volumes.

**June 6:** The internal version of Zip was introduced and immediately adopted by Power Computing Company as an option of its Macintosh clones.

**June 12:** Iomega tops the industry's price/performance standard with its announcement of the one-gigabyte Jaz drive and disks.

**June 21:** Seiko Epson Corporation teams with Iomega to dramatically increase production of Zip drives.

**July 5:** An agreement is announced with Wells Fargo Bank to provide Iomega with up to $60 million of credit to finance the company's rapid growth.

**September 18:** Iomega creates a new standard for value and performance in tape backup with the portable Ditto Easy 800 at under $150.

**November 8:** Micron Electronics, one of the fastest-growing computer companies in the U.S., announces it will offer Zip, Jaz and Ditto drives as factory installed options.

**November 13:** Iomega announces shipment of its one-millionth personal storage solution during calendar-year 1995.

**November 16:** Iomega Europe GmbH enters into a multi-currency financing agreement with Heller Bank for up to DM 50 million ($35 million U.S.).

**December 14:** Iomega announces plans for a 3-for-1 stock split.

**December 20:** Production shipments of the Jaz drive begin with internal versions going to key OEM customers in the audio and video industries.

During the year it became evident that we could sell close to a million Zip drives and about six million Zip disks. Such success resulted in an undesirable situation; customers had to wait several weeks for the products. We started Zip production with a two-shift, six-day schedule, and within a couple of months we instituted a three-shift, seven-day a week production capacity in Iomega's location in the United States. However, even this was inadequate to fulfill the demand. In the later part of the year we started Zip drive production in the Philippines and Zip disk production in Taiwan using local subcontractors.

The production facilities in the Philippines and Taiwan required close coordination with facilities in the US. It required additional tooling and test equipment to be built in the US and transferred to the subcontractors. It also required training the subcontractors' people as well as extended stays in the Philippines and Taiwan for our engineers. The logistics of parts shipments and receipt of finished products presented challenges to our procurement, materials control and logistics departments. Sometimes, in spare moments of contemplation, I wondered how the Persian Gulf War generals were able to cope with the logistical challenges of the day. I marveled and praised my subordinates, vice president of worldwide logistics and materials, Mr. Willard Kennedy and vice president of outsourcing, Mr. John Thompson.

The financial and operating highlights for 1995 were as follows (Figures taken from the 1995 Annual Report):

(Amounts in thousands except employee data)

|  | 1995 | 1994 |
|---|---|---|
| Sales | $326,225 | $141,380 |
| Gross margin | 90,387 | 48,927 |
| Selling, G&A | 57,189 | 36,862 |
| R&D Expenses | 19,576 | 15,438 |
| Operating income (Loss) | 13,622 | (882) |
| Net Income | 8,503 | (1,882) |
| Employees (year end) | 1,667 | 886 |

While 1995 was a year of real accomplishment, it was a challenging year from beginning to end. During the year it was virtually impossible to forecast revenues and manage our business to established goals. Our revenues were controlled by market demand on the one hand, and shortages of components on the other. We also had to manage enormous production growth with overseas subcontractors. In spite of this huge growth we managed to maintain the products high quality standards achieved in the previous years.

For me personally it was a challenge. It was filled with achievements and extremely satisfactory results, which I could have never attained without dedicated management and people in engineering, production and quality. Many a time they saved me from my follies and potential disasters. I shall remain grateful to the team as long as I live and remember this joyous ride.

# $\mathcal{C}$hapter XII

## On the Road to Retirement

During the year 1995, from time to time, I discussed my potential retirement with my wife. My reasoning was that the company was growing at a very fast pace and we needed new blood to manage this growth. During the year we hired a number of middle-level managers including some executives in all departments. I also felt that the operations needed a new outlook, although I was not tired, in good health, and felt that I would be able to contribute. However, I was over 68 years of age, had witnessed the birth and growth of the computer industry where I spent over 40 years of my career. I also helped to save Iomega from potential bankruptcy in 1987. I felt that a new outlook and fresh ideas in operations would be beneficial to the company's growth. Fran, my wife, agreed with me. Therefore, during the fourth quarter of 1995 I notified the Iomega president that I intended to retire on August 15, 1996, exactly nine years after joining the company.

After appropriate notification to the chairman of the board, I was told that I could stay with the company as long as I wished. This was a very generous offer, but I felt that if they hired a new chief operating officer, I should not interfere in his operating mode.

During the fourth quarter I started looking for my replacement. After sorting through a large number of resumes and a few interviews with the help of other executives and members of the board, a candidate was selected and started his job in January 1996.

1996 began the same way as the year 1995 ended; we were producing Zip drives and disks in record quantities and were selling all we could make. Also we were shipping Jaz drives and disks and Ditto tape drives in large production quantities.

## *The Philippines*

I was grooming my successor and showing him what I had done the prior eight-and-a-half-years. After about three months it was obvious that the new senior vice president of operations wanted to assert himself, which was fine with me. At that time a new challenge presented itself to me. In the Philippines there was a capable subcontractor for Zip drives, but they required technical support from Iomega Engineering. We sent a very capable and hard-working individual, Mr. Mike Lyon, who provided excellent technical support, however he did not aspire to manage the interface with the subcontractor and Japanese Epson Corporation. This interface was becoming urgent since we were working towards a partnership with Epson. Our president asked me if I felt comfortable with my successor's knowledge of operations, and if so, would I be willing to go to the Philippines for a period of time and establish a working relationship with Epson. I agreed and in the later part of March departed for the Philippines.

The work there was complicated because of the potential partnership with Epson, involvement of a local subcontractor and building of a new facility in the tax free zone, which was a designated tax free export location strongly controlled by the Philippine government. Needless to say, I had much to learn, very fast, in my daily dealings with Philippine government officials, potential Japanese partners and subcontractor management.

Work was very interesting yet sometimes frustrating when it required dealing with the building contractors and conflicting cultures of the Filipinos, Japanese and Americans. The other undesirable situation was living in a hotel located in downtown Manila. It was very modern and comfortable, but still it was a hotel, not a home. Fortunately, I spent only about four months there, with a couple of interruptions to travel to the United States for company meetings.

A pleasant diversion was my wife's and my secretary's visit to the Philippines and a few days of recreation in Singapore.

Work progressed satisfactorily. Mike Lyon was quite capable of dealing with production and technical issues and I enjoyed the occasional visit to the factory that was located about 25 kilometers from Manila. One necessary inconvenience was that we could not drive because the driving situation in Manila and surrounding areas was chaotic, to say the least, and it was not safe for an American to drive. Therefore, we were required to hire a full-time car and driver.

While in the Philippines, I had an opportunity to ride in the unique Philippines invention: the "Jeepney". The origin of this contraption was the discarded American jeeps after WWII. Enterprising Filipinos repaired these discarded jeeps, added wooden seats and used them as mini-busses. They were beautifully decorated with painted flowers and various other designs on the outside. There were no doors or windows in these vehicles, since the climate in the Philippines is summer all year round. The entrance to the vehicle was through the rear opening. After a few miles on dirt roads the passengers were quite dusty but reached their destination reasonably cheap. The "mini-bus" usually could comfortably seat 8-10 people, but when the business was good, an operator-driver managed to squeeze in 16-18 people. Nowadays they purchase especially designed chassis' for Jeepneys from Japan.

Working with the construction people that were building our factory in the tax-free zone was another new experience. First, the construction safety regulations were such that in the United States OSHA would shut down the construction and the builder would go to jail. There simply were no safety regulations. The workers wore no hard hats, many were barefoot and the scaffolding was constructed from bamboo sticks fastened with wire strings. When I questioned about the safety regulations, the answer was, we are safe enough. When I asked what would happen if a worker got injured or killed, I was told that for every one that falls into difficulty, there are several hundred who are willing to work under the conditions that exist.

The other peculiarity was that the worker's families moved with the workers. In our building, as soon as the roof was on, the worker's families including children moved under the roof. There around an open fire they cooked meals, washed clothes and dishes and slept, in other words, made their living quarters until the building was completed.

My workload became excessive, so I asked Mr. Travis Smith to come and help me in the construction of the building, which in itself became a full-time job. When seeing the safety situation he was as astonished as I was. Ultimately we accepted their work safety habits, but we were not happy.

I was making good progress regarding the partnership with Epson Corporation. In preparation to clarify the partnership working agreement I traveled to Suwa, Japan, Epson headquarters and brought in some experienced people from Roy, Utah. We created a working document from which we would prepare a final partnership document. We also were able to find a Filipino working in the United States and recruited him as general manager of this new partnership. Several Japanese nationals agreed to move to the Philippines, the location of the headquarters of this new entity.

I wanted to finish this work before August 15,

my planned retirement date. One day new information was submitted to me by several Iomega executives during their visit to Manila on the way to Malaysia. I was informed that they were traveling to Penang, Malaysia to review the potential purchase of an over 370-thousand-square-foot manufacturing facility. I wanted to know why we were contemplating purchasing the facility in Malaysia when we already were building a production facility in the Philippines. I was told that it was a very good price, approximately half of the appraised value of the property. I was skeptical, but not having any more information I kept my own council. When I came to Roy for our management meeting I had a long discussion with Mr. Kim Edwards, our president, and I questioned him about the potential purchase of the building in Malaysia. He showed me the model of the building and asked me what I thought of it. I told him that it "was a solution looking for a problem". Better stated it was a "monument" for my successor, Mr. Wayne Stewart, and his vice president, Mr. Reed Brown. In my opinion, they wanted to leave an imprint of their own on the company and to some extent disassociate their efforts apart from my legacy.

I questioned the wisdom of the purchase of Malaysia facility, since our arrangements in the Philippines were working just fine and we were able to deliver quality products at low cost from the Philippines. With the new building in the tax-free zone in the Philippines we would be in a position to deliver several billion dollars worth of products. I felt that the facility in Malaysia would require substantial support from Roy at the start of operations, expenses that did not need to be incurred when things were working fine in Philippines. Besides, I thought the Malaysian facility was much too large for our current and projected business needs for a few years. Mr. Edwards did not take my advice, because in the fourth quarter of the year, after my retirement, Iomega announced the purchase of the Malaysian facility. In July, I felt bad about the Malaysian situation but chose not to make a big issue about it since I had only about one month left before my retirement.

In retrospect, it appears that my position was a correct one. The Malaysian facility was never fully utilized. There were some management and line worker problems that required substantial support from Roy, Utah. As I understand, about half of the facility was empty for over six years. Finally, at the end of 2002, the facility was sold to Iomega's subcontractor in Singapore for less than half of the price paid originally by Iomega. After I retired, I heard that there were some difficulties and hard feelings with Epson, since in my judgment Epson did not receive a fair deal regarding the partnership in the Philippines. I also thought that our subcontractor in the Philippines was dealt a "bad hand" regarding the termination of their subcontracting business with Iomega. Of course, these deals were made after I retired.

## Final Career Accomplishments

In general, the year 1996 was quite successful. Although I retired in August, the president and the board of directors thought that my contribution was substantial and I received a very good bonus for the year.

The following are the financial and operating highlights of business during 1996 (Figures taken from the 1996 Annual Report):

(Amount in thousands except employee data)

|  | 1996 | 1995 |
|---|---|---|
| Sales | $1,212,769 | $326,225 |
| Gross Margin | 332,780 | 90,387 |
| Selling, G& A | 190,719 | 57,189 |
| R&D Expenses | 42,101 | 19,576 |
| Operating Income | 99,960 | 13,622 |
| Net Income | 57,328 | 8,503 |
| Employees (year end) | 2,926 | 1,667 |

The key milestones for the year were as follows:

**January 4, 1996:** Wayne Stewart named senior vice president, operations. Willard Kennedy named vice president, worldwide logistics and materials.

**January 8:** IomegaSmart tailored programs introduced to educators.

**January 9:** IomegaReady Imaging Bureau developed to provide Zip support to graphics professionals.

**January 24:** 4Q95 results: revenues of $148.8 million, net income of $9.9 million, annual sales $322.2 million.

**January 26:** 3-for-1 stock split announced.

**February 12:** Revolutionary tape line extended with Ditto Easy 3200.

**February 28:** Hewlett-Packard Company announced plans to incorporate Zip into Pavilion multimedia PC.

**March 8:** Public offering of convertible subordinated notes of $43 million announced.

**March 14:** Iomega shipped one million Zip drives in less than a year.

**April 18:** 1Q96 results: revenue of $222 million and net income of $10.1 million. Sony Pictures Entertainment entered into agreement for Jaz drives and disks.

**April 22:** Aggressive VAR initiative announced to support Iomega sales.

**April 23:** 2-for-1 stock split announced.

**April 30:** Agreement with Sentinel NV to manufacture Zip disks in Europe announced.

**May 9:** Iomega opened new Asia Pacific headquarters in Singapore.

**May 13:** $100 million credit facility announced with Wells Fargo Bank.

**May 23:** Packard Bell incorporated Zip into home PC line.

**June 3:** Three million personal storage solutions shipped; two million were Zip drives.

**June 10:** IBM announced adoption of Zip drive in Aptiva line of PCs.

**June 12:** Iomega completed $191 million equity offering. NEC proclaimed Iomega "emerging standard in removable storage".

**June 14:** Gateway 2000 agreed to offer Ditto Easy 3200 as option across entire line.

**June 18:** Additional Zip OEM agreement announced with Unisys. IomegaReady program announced, helping OEM and channel partners launch and sell Iomega-compatible systems.

15mm Zip drive for laptop computers unveiled. Zip-unleashed battery pack and PCMCIA adapter card set new standards for Zip mobility.

**July 1:** $50 rebate with a purchase of a Zip drive announced.

**July 3:** Jaz drive entered retail channel; price reduced to $399 for internal drives, $499 for external drives. Introduced "Jaz Jet" cross-platform PCI solution.

**July 18:** Iomega announced intent to purchase 376,000-square-foot Malaysian manufacturing site for all products. 2Q96 results: revenues of $283.6 million, net income of $14.1 million.

**August 5:** VST Technologies agreed to provide internal Zip drive for Apple PowerBook.

**August 6:** Jaz recognized as storage solution for consumer movies, using Avid Cinema software on Apple systems.

**August 23:** Iomega announced major enhancements in technical support.

**September 3:** Ditto 2 gigabyte (GB) (compressed capacity) introduced, setting new standards for backup capacity and price.

**September10:** Matsushita licensed to produce Zip drives, further establishing Zip as emerging floppy replacement.

**September 16:** Cannon announced support of Iomega storage solutions in OEM agreement.

**September 19:** Iomega announced Zip to be bootable from the A: drive.

**September 23:** New Zip tools software and internal 3.5" SCSI Zip drive unveiled.

**September 26:** "Zip-Across-America," a national education program, launched.

**October 1:** Iomega shipped three million Zip drives and five million personal storage solutions.

**October 17:** 3Q96 results: revenues of $310.1 million, net income $12.8 million. Douglas Clifford named vice president, research and development and chief technology officer.

**October 31:** Timothy Good is named chief information officer.

**November 1:** Shun Kaneko named director of strategic business development.

**November 4:** CNF Inc. plans to include Zip drive in Compaq LTE 5000 notebook computers.

**November 5:** New OEM partnership with Gateway 2000, including Jaz and Zip drives, announced.

**November 6:** Slimmer (12.7 mm) version of Zip drive announced for notebook computers.

**November 7:** Iomega introduced n*hand technology.

**November 8:** Iomega moved from NASDAQ to New York Stock Exchange.

**November 11:** VST Technology announced Zip drive for IBM Thinkpad computer models with the UltraBay.

**November 16:** Kim Edwards received the Ernst & Young, LLP National Entrepreneur of The Year Award in the turnaround category.

**November 18:** Zip incorporated into NEC Computer Systems' Versa notebooks.

New "IomegaReady" software, designed to auto-matically detect presence of Zip or Jaz drive announced.

**December 30:** Iomega announced that it shifted production from the Philippines to the Malaysian site. Iomega selected a new European headquarters in Geneva, Switzerland.

**January 8, 1997:** Compaq and Dell announced plans to incorporate Zip drives as an option on desktop PCs. Hewlett-Packard, Packard Bell, NE and Micron Electronics extended the availability of Zip in select versions of new MMX enabled PCs.

**January 9:** Gateway 2000 announced plans to offer internal Zip drives as an option on Desktop PCs.

**January 20:** Kevin O'Connor named vice president, human resources.

**January 28:** Iomega announced more than four million Zip drives sold. 4Q96 record results: revenues of $397.1 million, net income of $20.3 million (including one time charge), annual sales of $1.2 billion.

In my summary of our performance for the year in this book I used a normal, non-exaggerating language while the chairman of the board and the president used superlatives in their messages in the annual report for the year 1996. Since the results for the company were indeed outstanding by any measure, I can appreciate their enthusiasm, but in business one has to be careful, because the future is not always kind to current superlatives. In my later conversations with the chairman and the president I pointed out my reluctance to be over-optimistic. Future events in the company proved that my misgivings were closer to reality.

## *The First Day of Retirement*

August 15, 1996 dawned like many other August days in Utah; not a cloud in the sky, hot and dry. To me, however, this was a very special day: it was the cessation of my work at Iomega. This was the day that I cleaned out my desk and filing cabinets. Those items that were company property I left in the filing cabinet and desk drawers; those that were my personal property, I packed in cardboard boxes and carried to the car. There was nothing else to do, other than sit at the desk and wait for the retirement celebration lunch arranged by my faithful assistant for nine years, Mrs. Dolores Valdez.

While waiting for lunch I received many well wishers. They were my associates, coworkers in my departments and many from other departments. Mrs. Dolores Valdez prepared a "JOURNAL" with many pages of signed well wishes, numerous photos of the festivities including some humorous statements from several executives and a valuable gift, an expensive golf driver presented to me by my boss, our president, Mr. Kim Edwards. The most cherished photograph, prepared by Dolores, included all the secretarial assistants that worked in my departments, with an inscription as follows:

*"Some people come into our lives and quickly go. Others come into our lives and leave footprints on our hearts, and we will never be the same. Thanks for the memories and support".*

In the first paragraph of this section I stated that August 15 "was the cessation of my work at Iomega". I chose those words very carefully because, although I vacated my office on that day and never set foot in it again, I actually was on the payroll until December 17 due in part to accumulated vacations, unused sick leave, and part due to a board decision to extend my pay for a period of time. The following morning I got up later than usual and wondered what in the world I would do all day, not just that day but from that day forward, every day, until I would expire. Actually it was a gross miscalculation. As time passed my wife and I found ourselves busier than when I was working. Later we often wondered how we managed to get everything done when I was working. I believe that Fran carried much of the family work on her shoulders without me knowing anything about it. Actually life became very interesting. Read on!

## *My Back Operation*

For a number of years I had experienced back problems. Sometimes my back would flare up and I could hardly walk for a few minutes, then everything would be normal again. My wife urged me to go to a doctor, but I am not much of a visitor to doctors' offices and I stalled. I think my retirement accelerated the need to go to the doctor, because my wife noticed my discomfort and she is not one to ignore my physical pain. Finally I agreed to visit a back specialist, Dr. Donald Bryan, who had an office in Ogden. He was also an Air Force surgeon with the rank of general.

He gave me a thorough examination including an x-ray and told me that I had two ruptured disks and in order for me to eliminate my back pain I would need an operation. My wife, given the opportunity, asked the doctor if my smoking was harmful. The doctor, prompted by my wife's question, told me that I should quit smoking because he would be reluctant to operate on me unless I quit. At first I protested by asking what smoking had to do with a problem in my back. He patiently explained that nicotine permeates the blood stream and strongly suggested I quit smoking. I watched my wife with a gleam in her eyes, for she had been urging me to quit smoking for a long time. She probably was the happiest person not only in that office but probably in the whole medical complex of the hospital. I agreed with him and from that day onward to this day I have not had one cigarette. I used no medication or patches; it was strictly my will and determination to stop smoking.

When we arrived home from the doctor, my wife sent me out on some unneeded errand. When I came back home, the whole carton of cigarettes I had in the house was gone, including the lighters and matches. She also "confiscated" my unfinished pack of cigarettes and extracted promises that I indeed would quit smoking. Here I can say with all sincerity that the cigarette that I smoked in the parking lot before seeing the doctor was my last cigarette to this day. The only discomfort I experienced in quitting was that for a while I felt that after meals I did not know what to do with my hands. Contrary to many statements regarding the improved sense of smell and improved taste of food after one stopped smoking, I felt no improvement in these areas. I did, however, stop coughing at night.

I had two weeks to prepare for the operation including the extraction of two pints of blood in case it was needed during surgery. My procedure was on October 26, 1996. The operation was very successful and in four days I was discharged from the hospital. I healed well, needed virtually no pain killer medications and within a few days I was able to take a bath. The only problem was my wife. She hovered over me all day long asking what she could do for me. After a few days I told her that she should go shopping and leave me alone for a while, with not much success I might add.

After the first post-operative visit to the doctor, he told me that in a week or two I should be able to start driving a car and to continue my walking exercises. After six weeks I took a plane ride from Salt Lake City, Utah to Las Vegas, Nevada. After an additional four or five weeks, I was able to start playing golf. Since the operation I have not had any more pain in my back and to this day feel quite well. I used up my sick leave from Iomega for my several weeks of convalescence, hence as I mentioned earlier, that was the reason for the extended period on the Iomega payroll after my official retirement date.

## *Life in Retirement*

The proverbial saying that retirement is easy,

relaxed, with plenty of time for everything surely does not apply to Fran and me. Since my retirement we have been as busy, if not more so, than when I was working. Let me start at the beginning.

While I was still working, from time-to-time we discussed that we may want to move back to the East Coast after my retirement. We even purchased some land in Knoxville, Tennessee where we planned to build a house and be closer to Fran's parents. After contemplating for several months, we came to the conclusion that with the exception of Fran's relatives we had no close friends there, while in the Ogden, Utah area, we had a number of very close friends. With air transportation it takes but a few hours to reach Knoxville, from Ogden, which means that we can visit Fran's relatives on the East Coast anytime we want. Based on that reasoning, we decided that after my retirement we would stay in the Ogden area. After making this decision, we sold our property in Knoxville.

Since winters in Ogden can often be rather severe, we decided to build a winter home in Mesquite, Nevada, where the temperatures in winter are rarely below 50 degrees. Consequently, in March of 1996, we purchased a lot and started building a house on the 18th fairway of the Oasis Golf Course.

There is another advantage to being in Mesquite in the winter. The golfing is a year-round proposition. I am not the best golfer, but I like to improve my skill and reasoned that frequent golfing may help; at least that is what I thought. Our winter home in Mesquite, Nevada was completed in December 1996.

There was a learning process how to live in two homes. After furnishing the new house, we learned that there are other problems. It seems that every time we cooked something, suddenly we found that one item or another needed for the meal was not in the pantry. We remembered that it was in the "other" house. Now it has been over eight years, but we still occasionally forget something and blame it on the "other" house. What amazes me is how Fran was able to create aesthetically pleasant and comfortable living environments in two dissimilar climates, one seasonably changeable, relatively cold Northern Utah and another semitropical, desert conditions of Southern Nevada.

Since I was able to go golfing anytime, Fran entertained herself by reading books, or occasionally going to Las Vegas, which is only about 80 miles from our house. After about a year-and-a-half, we decided to build a swimming pool and a pool house (casita) next to our house. It is enjoyable swimming in summer and in winter.

## Giving Back to the Community

Although I have lived in the United States for over half a century, I still have emotional ties with Lithuania. When in February of 1993, I traveled to Lithuania for my mother's funeral I saw the church where I was an altar boy as it really was—not as I idealized from my imagination as a youth. When I was a boy, that little village church looked like the cathedrals of Europe to me.

In reality that little church was practically falling apart, primarily due to neglect during 50 years of Communist occupation of Lithuania. Sometime in 1997, I suggested to Fran that maybe we should help to repair and restore that little church in Plutiškės. Fortunately for me Fran agreed, although she had no emotional ties with Lithuania or that church, other than being married to me and having visited the country a few times.

Finding contractors and supervision of the work for the church restoration and repair was carried out by my cousin's son-in-law, Laimutis Marcinkevičius. He simultaneously had a full-time job as assistant post master in Marijampolė, which was about 15 miles away from Plutiškės.

The work on the church was completed in September 1998. The bishop of Vilkaviškis agreed to consecrate High Mass for this memorable occasion and the pastor invited several priests from surrounding parishes as guests. I, Fran, my in-laws, our children with their spouses and grand children traveled to Lithuania for this celebration.

The church was overflowing with worshipers. Fortunately the weather was pleasant, so that those who could not fit in the church were able to celebrate outside. Fran and I were invited to sit by the altar inside the gate. During the celebration the bishop gave Fran and me personal gifts from Pope John Paul II. We both treasure these gifts beyond anything that we ever received in our lives. The bishop explained the situation about the gifts as follows: When the bishop was in Rome on some church business, he told the Pope about this Lithuanian-American who was financing the restoration and repair of the small church where, as a boy, he was an altar boy. The Pope was moved and personally bestowed those gifts to Fran and me.

After the Mass, we were interviewed by several news media and had occasion to meet many of our relatives. The local middle school students staged a show in honor of the American guests. After the Mass, we invited our relatives, guests and contractors to a dinner at which time we received many gifts. The following days we were invited to numerous celebrations by my relatives and old grammar school classmate's homes. Every place we went we had to eat. In a given day we must have eaten seven or more times. That is Lithuanian hospitality! After this memorable visit, we, the American contingent, departed Lithuania.

When we reached Frankfurt, Germany, Fran and I decided to take my in-laws on a trip from Frankfurt all the way to Czekoslovakia, now called the Czech Republic. That route was the route that my father-in-law traveled, mostly on foot, when he was in the service during World War II. This, of course, was very memorable for my mother-in-law to see where her husband was during the war.

On the way back to Frankfurt, we stopped in Munich (Muenchen in German) to see some of the noted tourist places including the famous "Glockenspiel" and had the opportunity to partake in October Fest which was going on at that time. We all came home tired but with memories that will last us a lifetime.

Since we spent some money on my memories, I urged Fran to spend some money regarding her childhood memories. After reading an article in the Maryville, Tennessee paper about the need for thermal imaging cameras at the Blount County Fire Department, Fran decided to make a donation to the fire department. She called the fire department chief, Doug McClanahan, and offered him the donation. The fire chief was not only surprised but had a difficult time accepting Fran's offer as real. After all, who would call him from Utah and offer money. Of course, he changed his mind when Fran told him over the phone that she was coming to Tennessee and when would he be available to accept the check. The meeting date was set and at the designated time, Fran and I met the chief and a number of his assistants.

The fire chief's appreciative remarks and equipment demonstrations were reported by the local newspaper. Fran's picture appeared on the front page of the paper while the picture of the visit of President Bush was smaller and relegated to the next page. My father-in-law had a good chuckle about the fact that Fran outshone the president in terms of the size and the location of the pictures in the newspaper.

## *The 2002 Winter Olympics*

Sometime early in 2001, I met an acquaintance in one of Fran's favored charity balls, called the Eccles Community Art Center. He urged me to participate as a volunteer in the 2002 Winter Olympics. Since I can speak several languages he thought I could be useful. After considering his suggestion and discussing volunteer issues with Fran, I decided to enroll as a volunteer for the 2002 Winter Olympics.

After an interview I was accepted and was

asked to interview other potential volunteer candidates, since I already had substantial experience in interviews during my professional career. The interviews took place in Ogden, Utah once a week and lasted about three months. It was very interesting to hear people tell the reasons why they wanted to be volunteers. Some thought that it was an opportunity to do something worthwhile for the community, while others thought that it would be "neat" to mix with the athletes and some thought that this was a way to enter the Olympics for free. To those that wanted to see the Olympics for free I explained that volunteers would be assigned to a given location and depending on the assignment and shift, may not have an opportunity to attend a given venue for free. Some of them withdrew at that point while others, I do not think, believed me, so they didn't receive a favorable recommendation from me.

The first meetings of the volunteers were in Salt Lake City with Mr. Mitt Romney, chairman of the Salt Lake City Olympics Committee (SLOC) and Mr. Steve Young, former quarterback for the San Francisco football team, as honorary chairman of the volunteers. There were encouraging talks from both chairmen which effectively said that our work would be very important to the success of the Olympics, and the services for the athletes and visiting guests.

The generalized volunteer training was held in a facility near Ogden, Utah, where we were trained in general behavior, dress code, how to greet guests and athletes, what to say and what not to say. Questions that were specific were to be directed to the appropriate areas, such as news media questions to be addressed by the National Olympic Committee news room, etc.

Although initially I volunteered for the Lithuanian athletic team services, at the beginning of the specific training I was asked to become a NOC service center associate, since there were an adequate number of volunteers for the Lithuanian team, but inadequate number of volunteers in the NOC service center. Also, I had the advantage that I could speak several languages.

I agreed to this request and thus became a NOC Service Center associate. The NOC service center associates were based in the service center and were required to provide administrative and logistic support to individual country chiefs and SLOC functions based in the center. This job proved to be very interesting and highly rewarding. For me it was a ONCE IN A LIFETIME CHANCE. The tasks and responsibilities for the NOC Service Center associates were as follows:

- Provide general information services
- Sort and distribute mail, faxes, gifts, partici-

pation medals, pins and diplomas
- Provide office administration support to country chiefs
- Coordinate service center meeting room reservations
- Assist with lost and found issues
- Put together athlete welcome bags

Required knowledge/Skills/Certifications/Licenses/Language
- Verbal and written fluency in English
- Verbal and written fluency in a second language
- Experience working and/or living in an international setting
- Successful team involvement
- Excellent communication skills
- Knowledge of local community including traffic routes
- Clean law enforcement record
- Ability to learn and retain numerous details regarding specific programs, procedures and policies
- Positive, calm, flexible personality

Required Training
- General level volunteer training
- NOC and athlete services specific training

• NOC services center associates specific training

Comments/Recruiting Plan/Special Stipulations

Time commitment for the program included attending 2-4 hour monthly training sessions for up to 12 months prior to the games and the ability to volunteer for up to three weeks during the Olympic Games.

After training we received our uniforms, which were different in color depending on the assignments. For example, venue volunteers wore green, security wore yellow, medical support volunteers wore red and the service center associates wore blue. We also were issued passes, which were restricted to assigned areas. The service center volunteers received passes which allowed us to go to any venue or building.

All jobs in the service center were very interesting. Mail sorting by nationalities and distribution when requested by the country's representative, filling up welcome bags and distribution, registration of vehicles and assignment of vehicle keys and certification of driver's licenses, information desk duties and many non-recurring jobs, such as acting as an interpreter or assisting in travel arrangements made the shift go very fast. I worked second shift all 21 days that were needed. I had an opportunity to meet athletes of many countries and made friendships with many.

## *Adversities and Pleasant Life*

Our life was going in an idealistic fashion. We traveled a lot, visited our friends at Cape Cod and went sailing on their boat in the Caribbean, covering many islands. Then disaster struck! On the morning of June 7, 2003 we received a call from Fran's sister that their mother had suffered a brain aneurysm and was being rushed to University Hospital in Knoxville, Tennessee.

We hastily made arrangements to travel to Knoxville. When we arrived, we found mom in the critical care unit. After eight days she was moved to a regular hospital room and seemed to make improvements. On June 16 mom suffered a stroke. While still in the hospital mom had a feeding tube inserted after her stroke. A blood clot formed in her leg which necessitated that a filter be inserted in her artery. She was also diagnosed with sleep apnea.

She recovered and in August was moved to the Maryville Nursing and Rehabilitation Center. Her improvement was slow in coming. During this time, Fran made numerous visits to Tennessee. I traveled there as well. In February 2004, mom fell and broke her hip and cracked a rib. (The doctor did a partial hip replacement). Finally in July 2004, as Fran said, after one year, one month and one day, mom went home. Over the course of time, doctors found mom had breast cancer. Surgery was done a week later. She did not need chemotherapy or radiation. A complete success! The breast cancer and surgery happened so fast that it is hard to remember mom ever had cancer.

Next came a broken wrist, then a lot of pain in the hip that was broken. Fran made an appointment with mom's doctor, explaining all the pain mom was having and that she could hardly walk anymore. Within two weeks mom had a total hip replacement. Fran had told the doctor to do a complete hip replacement at the time of her first surgery, but he did not listen. After all, Fran has had both her hips replaced and knew what she was talking about.

Sickness in the Noel (my mother and father-in-laws) family was not limited to mom's problems. Dad had his problems with his back and knees. In January 2005, dad had a back operation. The problem was calcium build-up in the spine. The operation was a success and dad was able to walk within a few days.

The next problem was his knees. Although dad would not admit readily that his knees were in trouble, we knew how serious it was when he no longer attended the University of Tennessee football games, where he would have to walk at least a mile from and to the bus to reach the stadium seats. On May 12, 2005 he had a total knee replacement.

Although the operation was a success, the rehabilitation time was predicted to be long—up to six months before he would feel totally cured on that knee. Then the next knee operation would be made.

When our son David got married, he promised his wife, Jennifer, that someday he would take her to Lithuania. The opportunity arose in July 2004. Since neither David nor Jennifer could speak Lithuanian, I saw an opportunity to go as an interpreter. Fran, of course, decided to go along if for no other reason than to see Lithuania again and see our relatives. We arrived in Lithuania on July 3, 2004. Prior to arrival, I notified our relatives and the church pastor of our arrival and the desire to attend Mass in the Plutiškės church on July 4.

Everything went according to plan with the exception of our attendance in church. The pastor earlier announced our presence for that Sunday in church and arranged to have Bishop Norvila present. That was an honor we did not expect. After the service, we met privately with the pastor and the bishop for coffee and a discussion of church affairs. Afterwards we gave a luncheon for our relatives and guests, which was a pleasant interlude to see everyone and be together. At this point, I realized that my interpreting skills were not necessary for most of the Lithuanian youth spoke good English. Therefore, David and Jennifer did not need my help. Nevertheless it was pleasant to pretend that I was needed.

During our visit we rented a minibus and a driver and toured many noted places in Lithuania, such as: Kryžių Kalnas (Mount of the Crosses), Palanga and Neringa, two of the notable summer resorts, Kaunas and Vilnius monuments. It was also an opportunity to spend some time with the relatives, and as usual, eat and eat some more at their homes! Again, that is Lithuanian hospitality. On July 10th we departed for the United States with an overnight stopover in Copenhagen, Denmark.

In the ensuing years of my retirement, we learned how to cope with adversities and take in stride the pleasant life that we both enjoy. In retirement we have enjoyed travel, meeting relatives and friends, sampling various restaurants, visiting Fran's mom and dad and attending functions associated with my involvement in the local university.

## *Painful Interruption of a Pleasant Interlude*

Mom was diagnosed in February 2009 with lung, spine and pelvic cancer. Fran spent most of the first seven months of 2009 in Tennessee with her parents. I joined them in Tennessee every couple of months. Everything was going along well until June 2009.

We were in Mesquite, Nevada when Fran, talking to mom's caregiver, detected that everything was not OK with mom. I arranged for her to fly from Mesquite to Salt Lake City and arranged air travel for her the following day from Salt Lake City to Knoxville, Tennessee. She arrived at her parents about 2 p.m. on June 2nd, spending every minute with mom until the following morning at 3 a.m. when mom went to heaven.

The next day I made arrangements to travel to Tennessee. Fran, in spite of her grief, was able to help dad make arrangements for the funeral. After the funeral she stayed in Tennessee for about a month helping dad and her sister with some of the legal needs, and helping dad to adjust himself to a different life. I returned home a couple of days after the funeral.

Since mom's 89th birthday was on June 29th, dad wanted to commemorate her with a dinner with a couple friends and relatives. I traveled again to join Fran and dad for that joyous occasion remembering all of the wonderful times we had with mom. Another joyful occasion was dad's 90th birthday on July 21st. We had an open house to celebrate that wonderful milestone. At that time Fran convinced dad to visit us in Utah for a month.

On July 28th he traveled with us to Utah and stayed at our house until September 1st, when he and I returned to Tennessee. On September 5th dad and I went to the University of Tennessee foot-ball game. He has had season tickets for over 50 years. Such enjoyment certainly helps keep him active. I left Tennessee the following day knowing that dad was in good hands with caregivers.

For a period of time I was concerned about Fran's health although she bore her grief with an exceptional fortitude. To this day she still talks about mom with a painful expression on her face and an unsteady voice. However, time is a wonderful healer and I am certain she will overcome this grief, albeit it is impossible to totally forget a loving parent.

On December 19, 2009, Fran and I went to Tennessee to celebrate Christmas with dad and our son Stephen and his wife Lisa. Just to make dad's life more interesting we took a few days and traveled to Nashville, Tennessee, staying at the Gaylord Opryland hotel as well attended a beautiful show and lunch on the General Jackson cruise ship. We left him on December 28th and traveled to Dallas, Texas to visit our son David and our lovely daughter-in-law Jennifer. We celebrated the New Year with them returning to Utah on January 4th.

Fortunately, our life is getting back to normal, if there is such a thing. Occasionally we talk to our children on the telephone, exchange emails or have an opportunity to see them in person. We try to stay out of their business because they are all doing well in their chosen fields and we are happy for them. We again are looking forward to continuing our retirement.

# Chapter XIII

## Addendum

While living in the United States I contributed to Lithuanian causes and in a small way assisted my parents materially when possible, starting in 1957. In terms of causes for Lithuanian freedom I was a somewhat active member in local chapters of the Lithuanian-American Community of the USA, Inc. in Waterbury, Connecticut and Philadelphia, Pennsylvania.

When I was active in politics in Pennsylvania during the 1972 presidential elections, I was appointed as the director for immigrant minorities in Eastern Pennsylvania, where I actively encouraged minorities, especially in the Lithuanian communities around Philadelphia, to vote for Nixon as the next United States president.

In later years, particularly following the 1989 independence movement in Lithuania, I made numerous speeches on behalf of the Lithuanian situation. Following are some of my activities, speeches and interviews.

A. The Committee to Commemorate the 50th Anniversary of the Restoration of Independence to Lithuania.

B. A Day to Remember and a Lesson to Lead.

C. Letter to U.S. NEWS & WORLD REPORT.

D. Presentation to the Lithuanian-American Community of Philadelphia and Southern New Jersey.

E. Soviet Union, the Country of Contrasts.

F. Prophecies Fulfilled and some Advice for the New Year.

G. Quo Vadis Lithuania?

H. Local Lithuanians Watch the Developments.

I. Lithuanian Warns of Machiavellian Gorbachev.

J. Lithuania – Past, Present and Future.

# A. The Committee to Commemorate the 50th Anniversary of the Restoration of Independence to Lithuania

January 22, 1968

Dear friend and fellow Lithuanian:
One of the most significant events in the recent history of the Lithuanian nation took place in 1918, when the Lithuanians succeeded in re-establishing their independence and in founding the free democratic Republic of Lithuania. Now, in 1968, we are preparing to commemorate the fiftieth anniversary of this momentous event.

Our brothers and sisters who are still living in the motherland of Lithuania are unable to commemorate this anniversary in appropriate form since they are prevented from so doing by the Soviet occupation forces. We Lithuanian-Americans, however, who are living in the free democratic United States of America have not only the right, but even the duty to commemorate the fiftieth anniversary of this great event and at this opportunity to tell the world once again how terribly the entire Lithuanian nation is suffering under the Communist occupational regime and how strong the desire for freedom is.

The Lithuanian American Community of the U.S.A., Inc., Philadelphia and South New Jersey Chapters, have formed a special committee to commemorate this anniversary and this committee is in the process of organizing commemorative exercises, art exhibits, TV and radio programs and a number of other events about which you are being informed in a separate attachment to this letter. We do hope that you will consider it your duty and privilege to attend all of these planned activities.

One of the most important events will be a banquet, which the Lithuanian-Americans are organizing, along with the Estonians and Latvians, their old neighbors from the Baltic Sea.

The banquet and Friendship Ball is scheduled to take place on the ninth day of March, 1968, at 7:30 P.M., in the grand Ballroom of the Sheraton Hotel (1725 J. F. Kennedy Blvd., Philadelphia, Pa.).

To this banquet the organizers have invited a number of prominent and high ranking guests: the diplomatic representatives of all three Baltic countries in Washington, the Hon. Raymond Shaefer, governor of the Commonwealth of Pennsylvania, members of the U.S. Congress and other well known Americans. The program of the banquet provides for: greetings, main address, honoring of those Americans helping the cause of Lithuania, a concert of folk dance and music, and, finally, dancing until 1:00 A.M.

It is vital to the success of this banquet that as many Lithuanian-Americans as possible attend it. Therefore, the organizers extend a cordial invitation to you, to members of your family and your friends to come to this banquet. Tickets at ten dollars per person can be ordered in advance.

It is our sincere hope that you will find it possible to come to the banquet, thereby not only assuring yourself of an interesting and pleasant evening, but also helping the Lithuanian cause.

S.A. Gecys

Committee Chairman

J.A. Stiklorius

President,

Lithuanian-American Community of the U.S.A. Inc.

Philadelphia Chapter

NOTE: My participation in this commemoration was the draft of this letter and sale of tickets to the event.

263

## B. **A Day to Remember and a Lesson to Learn**

To most Americans, February 16th is just another day. However, to a handful of Americans of Lithuanian origin, February 16th is a day to remember. On this date in 1918, Lithuania declared restoration of its independence. At that time the independence movement in Europe was not like the independence movements in the sixties. There were no countries extending technical and economic aid to the new independent nations. In fact, the crumbling empires of Europe were determined not to let the small new nations be independent. Lithuanians lost over five percent of their people fighting, but they preserved their independence. They fought with inferior weapons, but superior will against formidable forces in Europe. Communist Russia was one of the enemies.

Although the freedom was short, 1918 – 1940, many things were accomplished by this industrious, small Lithuanian nation; illiteracy was almost wiped out, the economic position and the overall welfare of the people improved.

On June 15, 1940, Soviet Russia became the aggressor and the oppressor of this small nation and remains so until the present. Despite decades of cruel oppression, the spirit of this nation has not broken. Quite the contrary, it has been steadfastly

264

preserved without even the spotlight of history to encourage it. It should be remembered that from 1944 to 1953 Lithuanians fought guerrilla warfare against the overwhelming Soviet forces. After the soviets swept across Lithuania in pursuit of the crumbling Nazi German armies, Lithuanians took up arms. Small, highly organized, supremely disciplined groups of guerrillas thwarted the Soviet plans within Lithuania. These small, steel-nerved groups assassinated Soviet terror masters which were sent to subdue their nation. At no time did they delude themselves into believing that they could drive the soviets out of their nation. Their objective was rather to harass, to delay and to attract the attention of the West. Above all, to remind the people of the free world that they were victims of aggression, not partners in the Soviet "glorious state".

The world, however, closed their eyes and turned a deaf ear to the valiant but losing battle. Today, most of its guerrilla members killed, the remainder like shadows absorbed into the population, live under the ruthless oppression of the Soviet Russia. The political situation in the world today is not conducive to hopes for a quick solution and sympathetic approach to Lithuanian independence.

Remembering this February 16th, about one

million Americans of Lithuanian lineage have no cause for parades or plays, they just hope and pray. They hope that the supreme sacrifices of those thousands of young men that died in the independence war of 1918 and in the guerrilla warfare from 1944 to 1953 will not go unheeded. They pray for those men, women and children who resisted the oppression and died and are still dying in Siberian concentration camps.

So, remembering this February 16th, all people of good will should realize that the so-called peaceful world of today is by far not perfect and not peaceful. There are nations, like Lithuania, Latvia and Estonia, which proved their worth to be free, but are yet suppressed. They ask not that the democratic countries of the world give them economic and technical assistance or protect them with military power, they only ask the democratic powers of the world that their small nation be able to maintain its independence, be worthy to be in the family of free nations of the world, and they are asking these democracies of the world to help them restore their freedom again.

The Lithuanians have but one effective weapon in this endeavor and that is their untiring determination to turn to the free nations and to tell them about the plight of their small country on the Baltic Sea. They wish to tell the free nations of the world that they still desire to be independent and to tell them that they have determination, courage and the will to fight until Lithuania becomes independent again.

We Americans of Lithuanian lineage have the desire and are willing to be good citizens of this country, but we also wish our government representatives to know that our brothers and sisters in Lithuania, who live under oppression now, wish to be free and good citizens of Lithuania, a country restored under democratic principles, by the people, and for the people.

REMEMBER THOSE WHO LOST THEIR FREEDOM – APPRECIATE IT!

NOTE: This article was written by Leon Staciokas and was published in the local, Philadelphia-area newspaper on February 16th, 1970.

## C. Letter to U.S. NEWS & WORLD REPORT.

Leon J. Staciokas
1 Woodmont Drive
Downingtown, PA 19335

Mr. David Lawrence, Editor
Sept. 20, 1971
U.S. NEWS & WORLD REPORT, INC.
2300 N Street, N.W.
Washington, DC 20037

Dear Mr. Lawrence,

An article entitled "THE RUSSIA THAT AMER-ICAN TOURIST SEE" which appeared in the September 20, 1971 issue of your magazine gave me a lot of thought. My concern is not that the portion of the article entitled "Working to Correct Deficiencies" written by Professor Rezazadeh is misleading, but the fact that the article was written by a professor and a chairman of the Political Science Department is what disturbs me most. One can not help but feel very uncertain about our youth because they are being taught by such men as Professor Rezazadeh, who lacks candor, objectivity and good judgment.

## Addendum

Professor Razazadeh's main guilt, as I see, is in the error of omission. It is indeed true that the apartments in the Soviet Union cost from $4.00 to $9.00 per month as compared to $150.00 in the United States. It is further true that a child's care is only $4.50 per month in a child care center. So when you consider that the average Russian is making $83.00 per month, it appears that the life in the Soviet Union is not that bad after all. What he neglects to mention is that a pair of shoes for the average Russian costs about $20.00, and that it takes about $60.00 per month to pay for his food. So when you add all of these essentials together, specifically the food and the clothing, there is hardly any money left for that inexpensive rent.

How can Professor Razazadeh, who also says that he is well versed in economics, be so one-sided and blind to the surroundings around him? He mentions nothing about the guides who are also KGB agents, nothing about poor public accommodations, nothing about the fact that you have to wait up to three hours in a restaurant to get a meal only to find out that the choice is not available even though it is on the menu and the constant surveillance of each individual, not to mention the fact that you have to pay in hard currency such as US dollars for the whole trip before you even step on the plane des-

269

tined for Moscow.

His stay of three weeks and covering several thousand miles does not make him an expert and, I think, that you are terribly negligent to the American public for allowing such shallow articles to be printed in your otherwise fine magazine.

Respectfully yours,

## D. Presentation to the Lithuanian-American Community of Philadelphia and Southern New Jersey. (June 11, 1972)

Highly respected Priests, Mr. Chairman, Dear Fellow Countrymen and Countrywomen!

With the passage of time, important events fade in our memories. Of course, there are exceptions. One such exception, to those that live here in the United States, is the June 1941 arrests and deportations to Siberia of our countrymen by the Soviet government. Everyone that was affected by those events to this day remembers well the place and the hour when he/she learned that their relative, friend or coworker was arrested. This was an unheard-of brutal act directed towards innocent people. Later, during the war and after the war, we heard even more reports of the brutal and barbaric genocide of people. However, not being direct witnesses to these events, we could only feel sympathies to the unfortunate. From such a perspective today we also look into the events that affected us in June, 1941.

Brothers and sisters in our native land remember less about that June, because after the war they lived through much more brutality lasting several years, arrests and deportations to Siberia. In Lithuania, also our neighbors Latvian and Estonian, the deportations between 1945 and 1950 were an unheard of harm inflicted by a stronger neighbor on a weaker one.

A couple of weeks ago I came back from the Soviet Empire where I spent about a month. In such a short time it is impossible to learn the details of people's lives and their feelings. However, in order even superficially to see and feel their lives would require hours of explanation. I will try, albeit abbreviated, to describe the ebb and flow of life there, of which, living here, we understand very little correctly.

We were permitted to stay in Vilnius only five days; we were not permitted to leave the boundaries of the city. Officially it is said that there are not enough hotel accommodations in Vilnius, therefore tourists are permitted to stay only five days. That is not the truth, because on the same floor where I stayed, only two rooms were occupied during that time.

Today Vilnius is about 35-40% Russians; it is the largest Russian contingent in a major Lithuanian city. It is said that Kaunas is more Lithuanian than Vilnius. The housing, as all other necessities of life, is of very poor quality. From the distance the living blocks do not look too bad, but close up the poor quality is visible. The interior of these multistory buildings is even worse than the exterior; it is indescribable. Even under such conditions the people have to wait four-five years to get such apartments. The sports stadium is the only beautiful, interesting building.

The service is terribly bad, however, that is not only in Vilnius, the same situation is all over the Soviet Union. The dislike of the Russians is big. Such a dislike is not shown openly, but quietly and passively people resist. For example, the service given to a Russian is worse than to the native Lithuanian. Life in general is drab and gloomy like a late autumn day. The quality of clothing is poor, the store windows empty. Alcoholism in Lithuania is lower than in Moscow or Leningrad, but still considerably high. It is the only "river" where Lithuanians can drown their sorrows and there are many of them.

While in Lithuania I heard from living witnesses the Golgotha roads that our country people trod and still tread to some extent.

After the war years the events in Lithuania have to be divided into three distinct phases: the first five years after the war; the following decade (about between 1950 and 1960) and the time between 1960 to this day.

THE FIRST FIVE YEARS AFTER THE WAR:

That was partisan activity, forced carrying out of individual farmers into collectives ("kolkhoz" in

273

Russian) and the massive deportations to Siberia. At that time there were three groups of partisans:

A) Forest brothers or "greens" – those were the men that fought and sacrificed themselves for ideals. To this group belonged men of strong will, uncommon courage and high discipline – heroes of our nation. Almost without exception, they died with a weapon in their hands fighting in an uneven fight for Lithuanian freedom.

B) The second group, which later attached themselves to the "greens," were men who faced jail or Siberia for the service in the military during the war opposing the soviets or the refusal to join the Red Army. They also distinguished themselves with courage and high discipline. Most of this group received a similar fate as the first group.

C) The third group – were robbers and thieves, who, using the uncertainty and disorder and covering themselves with the name of courageous partisans robbed, plundered and killed innocent Lithuanian people. Only a small number were killed accidentally, some were caught and punished, but most of them melted into the population or dispersed into wide Russian lands.

The deportations to Siberia were conducted without any consideration or reason. The deportees

were wealthy farmers, business owners,
well-off people, intelligentsia, small fa
were resisting forced entrance into c
("kolkhozes" in Russian) and completely innocent
people that were denounced by others, so to speak
to "get even". Large portions of the deportees
came back to Lithuania. Those that came back with
reasonable health, started life anew according to the
present expression "adjusted themselves to life since
life does not adjust to them". Many, however, came
back in poor health and today already departed this
world, while some, crippled physically and mentally,
are just waiting to die.

THE FOLLOWING DECADE (1950 – 1960):

This decade was the Lithuanian economic
agony. In the newly formed farm cooperatives
(kolkhozes) gross negligence reigned; shortages
of all types of farm implements, lack of fertilizers,
productivity was less than half what it was prior to
cooperatives and only half what it is today. Even
today's farm productivity is only a fraction of what
it is in the United States. Just the "plot-farmers"
saved Lithuanian farming from bankruptcy. The
plot-farmer was the member of the kolkhoz.

To the non-Lithuanian reader an explanation
of "plot-farmer" is in order. *When the farmers were
forced into the cooperatives and their land was confiscated*

were wealthy farmers, business owners, reasonably well-off people, intelligentsia, small farmers that were resisting forced entrance into cooperatives ("kolkhozes" in Russian) and completely innocent people that were denounced by others, so to speak to "get even". Large portions of the deportees came back to Lithuania. Those that came back with reasonable health, started life anew according to the present expression "adjusted themselves to life since life does not adjust to them". Many, however, came back in poor health and today already departed this world, while some, crippled physically and mentally, are just waiting to die.

THE FOLLOWING DECADE (1950 – 1960):

This decade was the Lithuanian economic agony. In the newly formed farm cooperatives (kolkhozes) gross negligence reigned; shortages of all types of farm implements, lack of fertilizers, productivity was less than half what it was prior to cooperatives and only half what it is today. Even today's farm productivity is only a fraction of what it is in the United States. Just the "plot-farmers" saved Lithuanian farming from bankruptcy. The plot-farmer was the member of the kolkhoz.

To the non-Lithuanian reader an explanation of "plot-farmer" is in order. *When the farmers were forced into the cooperatives and their land was confiscated without compensation, they were allocated a small plot, about ½ acre, on which they planted potatoes, vegetables and kept a cow, maybe a sheep and a few chickens. Their productivity was such that they were able to supply over three times the amount of dairy products compared to the newly formed co-operatives.*

From the moral standpoint the people were mortally wounded. The occupier destroyed what was dear to the Lithuanian people, such as the Tomb of the Unknown Soldier, the Three Crosses in Vilnius, where there grows meager grass and a few small pines. Many churches, especially those with distinguished unusual architecture or internal beauty, were converted into museums or warehouses. Today in Vilnius there are only 14 churches and one synagogue.

At the end of this decade the terror diminished and as a result the people began to renew themselves. The youth began to seek higher education, the economy began to improve, the cities destroyed in the war began to be rebuilt, the local culture revived, Lithuanians began to reinvigorate their national consciousness. In other words, this was a spiritual renaissance.

THE TIME FROM THE 1960s TO THE PRESENT:
Sometime during the decade of the 1960s the

I personally think we should also follow this example.

The strong and brutal hand of the occupant is felt all over. There is no free press or free speech, people cannot freely, without fear to go to church, often times cannot represent themselves as Lithuanians in foreign lands, and cannot travel freely abroad. The Communist system with its bureaucracy and inefficiency prevents improvements in living standards at the same rate as the Western world. Smiles and happy faces are very rare occurrences in today's Lithuania.

Nevertheless, in spite of these difficulties the Lithuanians are working, creating, fighting for their rights, in other words they are marching forward. Today there are more Lithuanians in responsible positions than there were in 1960. Lithuanians have developed a high cultural awareness; especially our sports people. Lithuanians are not broken physically or morally. They rejoice in their achievements and wish that we would rejoice as well. Let us be thankful to our country's men and women for their forbearance, work and resistance to the occupier. Let us help them not only materially but also morally. Their achievements should be acknowledged by us with the words that are so popular there today: "THE LAND THAT IS CALLED LITHUANIA".

## Addendum

The original presentation was prepared and made in the Lithuanian language by Leon Staciokas to the Lithuanian community of the Philadelphia area on June 11, 1972.

## E. Soviet Union – The Country of Contrasts

## Lecture Presented to the Lions Club in West Chester, PA by Leon Staciokas
## January 6, 1973

After President Nixon's visit to the USSR last year, the news media has been informing the American public about the "Great Bear" – our only worthy adversary. In spite of that information, to many American people the Soviet Union is still a mystery wrapped in enigma and encased in paradox. To some of us, who had occasion to work and study there, or had a reason to visit the country for a longer period of time the mystery is no longer there.

Last year, my wife and I spent a month in the Soviet Union. We made a visit for two reasons: to visit my parents and other relatives in Lithuania whom I had not seen for 28 years and possibly to arrange the export of US manufactured computers and related equipment.

The Soviet Union is a country of contrasts: at international forums their officials speak as defenders of freedom for all, while internally it is a prison of nations. Technologically they have made spectacular achievements in space, yet on earth cannot provide sufficient consumer goods for their own people. The country that contains the most fertile land in the world cannot feed its own people. Officially and in theory the country is ruled by a committee called Presidium, but in reality it is ruled by one man who does not even hold an official government post. (Brezhnev is the general secretary of the Central Communist Party, a post similar to the chairman of the National Republican or Democratic parties in this country.)

If one listens to Soviet radio broadcasts and reads newspaper articles, one gets the impression that life in the USSR is literally paradise. According to Soviet propaganda their people live in total freedom, an ideal classless society, and are provided for in every way. Everyone has his or her beloved hobby and well paid job, all have plenty of food and can live freely in the part of the country they choose in more than adequate quarters and have opportunities to have recreation unparalleled to any other place in the world. Therefore, all the people adore their government and support it fully and unceasingly chant praises to the Communist Party and its leaders, who are considered almost demigods.

Communist newspapers in the free world, amply subsidized from Moscow, spread this type of propaganda abroad which is intended for naïve people, who unfortunately are the majority in the free world. However, people who have escaped from that "paradise" or visited their relatives there and had the opportunity to talk to them, come back with a very different view on the Soviet Union. Some of the underground publications from the Soviet Union reaching the Western World portray a life over there that parallels that of Dante's "Inferno". In reality, the working class in the Soviet Union has no rights, are totally at the mercy of the administration, be it in industry or on the farm.

People are dissatisfied with the unequal distribution of goods, low wages, lack of housing, shortage of consumer goods of any type and being virtually tied down to their job at the government's pleasure. In reality the Soviet bureaucracy is stronger than that of the Czar's regime with a class distinction which far exceeds anything imaginable in the Western World. Such is the Soviet Union in real life!

The daily life of the majority of Soviet people is drab and without purpose. Total and absolute control of the economic life permits no private enterprise. The Soviet economy is not based on supply and demand principles as in the free enterprise system that we know, but it is planned and controlled by the all powerful "Gosplan" (the Central Planning Committee). Even such items as to how many pairs of shoes will be produced in a given year is planned in Moscow by the Gosplan. The labor unions, as we know them, are nonexistent. The so-called workers associations, which are organized along the line s of trades and professions, in reality are the tools of the government to meet their prescribed quotas of production. There is no such thing as negotiated wages and benefits; strikes are illegal! The wages as well as production quotas are set by the central planning function and passed to the various republics. (These are something synonymous to our states.) The administrators in these republics are permitted to deviate somewhat from the quotas, which accounts for the small variations in wages and the standard of living in the various republics. At this point I would like to mention that the country, which is the second industrial power in the world, has a standard of living which is 26th in the world of nations. On the average it takes about 200 rubles per month to support a family of four while the average worker earns about 150 rubles a month.

Promotions are not based on performance but rather on the activities and faithful service to the Communist Party. There is no incentive to do a good job because it will not be rewarded with money or advancement. Since everybody must work—the government says so—a person can hardly get fired for loafing. A change in job, which today is permissible, is a fruitless exercise because the next job in the same category will pay about the same regardless of where it is. Job change from one field into another is rather complicated and difficult.

Nowhere is the slow pace of the worker more apparent than in the service industries. For example, the service in restaurants is unbelievably bad; it takes two to three hours to complete a meal even though there may be five tables occupied with 15 waiters present. In the factories, where the work speed is often controlled by a machine, (ah, that capitalist invention), the worker must work at a certain pace. But the machine does not control quality; hence a 100% quota of shady goods is the norm. Since there is no incentive for performance, the productivity per worker is less than half compared to the United States.

Public utilities, such as transportation, entertainment places such as stadiums, contain minimum comforts and have only the bare essentials, but they function well and are very inexpensive. The trains, subways and planes are on time. Public telephones—functioning marginally at best—are in abundance in contrast to very few private phones. There is not a single telephone book in Moscow or any other major city in the Soviet Union.

Some of the areas that the government deems to be important are as good and in some cases better that in the United States. The medical care is adequate, free and accessible to all. They may lag in

284

modern equipment but that is made up in persever-
ance.

Education is compulsory up to the tenth grade
and the study of foreign languages is a must. Cities
are clean with well manicured parks and the streets
are safe. (I know, my wife and I walked Moscow,
Leningrad and Vilnius streets as late as two o'clock
in the morning without being molested.)

Although technologically the Soviet Union is
behind the United Sates by 10 to 15 years, the state
planned and controlled economy can achieve spectacular results, such as space exploration, military
preparedness and foreign assistance where the government sees some political gains. And, of course, I
must mention the beautiful and priceless museums.
The splendor and wealth that was taken away from
the tsar's family and the wealthy after the revolution
were converted into museums and are being taken
care of to this day. They are the pride and joy of the
country and rightfully so.

A businessman intending to trade with the Soviets will encounter intelligent, knowledgeable and
tough negotiators. He will also find impenetrable
bureaucracy and slowness that seems to be forever. He will be faced with many strange ways of
doing business in terms of meeting arrangements,
decision makers, payments and credits. Remember,
the Russian currency is not convertible in the

world banking industry; in other words, it's "funny money" for domestic use only. It is advantageous if you can speak, read and write Russian. Moscow and Leningrad streets signs are in Russian and the Russian alphabet is quite different from English. If a businessman learns how to cope with all these differences, he can have a rewarding and profitable business association. The Soviets honor their commitments once you make a deal.

As for the police state, the Soviet Union is definitely that. No free press, no free assembly, no criticism of the government or the Communist Party. Such opposition is considered state crime and dissenters are punished very severely. In spite of this there is a certain amount of opposition to the government stemming primarily from the scientists, writers, scholars and some students. The Soviet people have no say whatsoever about the choice of their government; the election process there is a fraud and a farce. They have no privilege of free elections as we do; if they did, I am sure, they would not abuse it as we do.

To foreign visitors the official representatives are courteous, reasonably well organized and are eager to please. It is likely that the visitor is being watched and listened to. If you are visiting the Soviet Union it is best to refrain from making derogatory remarks about the state or the government even in the privacy of your hotel room; one never knows when he/she may be overheard.

Russians themselves, who comprise about one-half of the total USSR population, are friendly, attentive and fun loving. Presently their biggest fun is getting drunk. The drinking problem there is more acute than the drug problem in this country. The other half of the population consists of about 150 different ethnic people groups. There are15 republics each having a different official language and culture. Some of the republics, such as my own native land Lithuania, have a long history and culture that is totally different from Russia. There is no such thing as the brotherhood of nationalities as the official Soviet propaganda would lead you to believe. In fact, the rivalry of the non-Russian republics against the Federated Russian Republic, (the ethnic Russian or the Big Brother) is severe, very real and subtle.

Movement of people within the Soviet Union is not restricted, but for an average Soviet citizen to leave the country either temporarily or permanently is an impossible dream. Some of the other impossible dreams are: to own an automobile, to own a house, become wealthy or to be a free person. The Communist functionaries, the scientists and the government officials have all the amenities of life that we are familiar with. Consequently, the so called "classless society" that Karl Marx envisioned and Lenin tried to create is non-existent. The difference between the privileged few and the oppressed many is very real in the Soviet Union today. If the government opened the borders for their citizens, literally millions would leave. The fact that at the end of the Second World War hundreds of thousands fled their homelands before the oncoming Communist armies and refused to go home after the war, speaks eloquently about life under communism. I am such a refugee myself.

Ladies and gentlemen, the contrast between the United States and the Soviet Union is so enormous, that it defies description. Although the average American knows very little about the USSR, the average Russian knows even less about the US.

I hope that after my remarks today you will not be so perplexed about this mystery wrapped in enigma and encased in a paradox, the country known as the Soviet Union.

Thank you for your indulgence.

REMARK: I gave the same presentation to the Rotaries Club of West Chester, PA on May 2, 1973.

# F. Prophecies Fulfilled and Some Advice for the New Year

At the end of the year it is customary for prognosticators and prophets to draw comparisons to their predictions at the beginning of the year, particularly if they are close to being right. The man who could make the most poignant comparisons to his predictions is no longer amongst the living; he is George Orwell, the author of the book "NINETEEN EIGHTY FOUR" written in the late thirties. Orwell's vision of totalitarian terror under **Big Brother** becomes more relevant as 1984 draws to a close. The "Newspeak" phrases of the book include:

WAR IS PEACE
FREEDOM IS SLAVERY
IGNORANCE IS STRENGTH

And multitudinous variations are being used throughout the world in all the vivid horror by the Soviet created and/or supported governments and agencies. Here are some examples:

*The United Nations Educational, Scientific and Cultural Organization (UNESCO), that spends 80% of the $200 million yearly budget on the maintenance of their Paris headquarters, is devoting most of what is left of the resources to such activities as the Soviet-inspired "collective rights" and "peace and disarmament" programs.

The so called "collective rights" are designs by the communists to restrict individual rights and freedoms recognized in the "Universal Declaration of Human Rights". The "peace and disarmament" activities are nothing more than Soviet-supported demonstrations and disruptions against the deployment of cruise missiles to defend Western Europe. The UNESCO move to create a government-controlled "new world information and communications order" which among other things would license journalists, is nothing more than an attempt to control freedom of the press.

*The Soviet invasion of Afghanistan and the slaughter of hundreds of thousands of that country's citizens and patriots during the last five years is masqueraded as the "invitation of the fraternal socialist government of Afghanistan to render assistance to rid the country of bandits, undesirable elements and foreign interference". That "fraternal socialist government" is a repressive gang of minorities supported by Soviet bayonets.

## Addendum

*The fermenting of revolutions to establish Communist dictatorships in El Salvador, Nicaragua, Angola, Morocco, Zimbabwe (Rhodesia) is proclaimed as "moral assistance to the capitalist-colonialist exploited proletariat masses".

*The dissidents of oppressive Communist government policies and human rights activists in the Soviet Union and their satellites are labeled as "hooligans, parasites and mentally unbalanced". They are summarily arrested, and many placed in psychiatric hospitals where they are injected with mind- and body-crippling drugs and ruined for the rest of their remaining natural lives.

*The economic bankruptcies of the old and the newly established Communist dictatorships are explained as success by "Big Brother" to their underfed, under-clothed and oppressed citizens. In a recent "Pioneer" publication (Soviet magazine for youth) a local educator explained to his perplexed little brood why Soviet stores were empty while those in the capitalist countries were full. "People in the capitalist countries do not earn enough money to buy products and therefore they remain on the shelves; the income of the Soviet people has been rising steadily so that now they can buy everything they desire. It is the buying power of the Soviet people that keeps the store shelves empty". How is that for a "Newspeak"?!

The perpetrators of the Nazi crimes during the Second World War were tried as criminals and received their due punishment. The perpetrators of the "Newspeak" crimes are being sought after and invited to the councils of civilized governments and even praised. Mrs. Thatcher recently said that she likes Mr. Gorbachev and she thinks they can do business together. Gorbachev recently was in England peddling the "immorality" of space defense weapons. Soviets do not want any defense against their formidable store of intercontinental ballistic missiles. Without the ICBM treaty how would they intimidate and blackmail the civilized world. Remember, Gorbachev is from the same "nice folks" that gave us Gulag Archipelago and, at the outset of the Second World War divided Eastern Europe with Hitler. Hitler's defeat negated what he gained by these nefarious deeds, while the Soviets kept it all and added some more since.

Western corporations are falling over each other to do business with the communists. Our banks extend such credit and terms to the communists, that if the same terms were extended to potential business partners in the West, they would be labeled as insane. Lenin, the creator of the "Newspeak" philosophy and deeds, once stated bluntly that communism will hang the capitalists. When he was politely reminded that Russia had no rope, Lenin very astutely observed that "capitalists will sell it to us on credit".

At the end of this 1984, we should learn again the Good Old English and be able to distinguish from the "Newspeak"; let us be aware who is wishing us what in the New Year.

NOTE: This article was written by Leon Staciokas on December 27, 1984 for the newspapers published in the Trenton, NJ area.

## G. Quo Vadis Lithuania?
## Presented to Utah State University
## By Leon Staciokas
## February, 1990

HISTORICAL PERSPECTIVE:

Lithuania, one of the three Baltic republics, traces its written history back to the first century when the Roman historian Tacitus described the tribes on the east coast of the Baltic Sea as traders in amber. Lithuanian tribes were united in 1251 by Mindaugas, the Grand Duke, who in 1253 became Lithuanian king. By the end of the 14th century the country stretched from the Baltic to the Black Sea, encompassing large parts of today's Ukraine, Bielorussia, Russia and Poland. In 1559 Lithuania entered into a union (Commonwealth) with Poland. Soon afterwards the union proceeded on the road of irredeemable decline. Mismanagement of the country's affairs, a decay of nobility and the tragic VETO power by the members of the Commonwealth (United Kingdom) parliament plus the never-ending wars with Russia and Sweden weakened the country to the point that by the later part of the eighteenth century the three major neighbors, Russia, Prussia and Austro-Hungary were annexing parts of the Commonwealth (United Kingdom) at will. In 1795, the final partition took place, at which time almost all of today's Lithuania became part of the tsarist Russian empire and the country ceased to exist.

Lithuanians resisted the occupation: there were uprisings in 1831, 1863 and 1905. Each time the Russians brutality suppressed the uprisings with a loss of life and deportations to Siberia. At the end of the First World War in 1918, Lithuania declared independence and proclaimed itself a democratic republic. On July 20, 1922, Lithuania signed a peace treaty with Russia and Lenin himself renouncing all rights for all times to Lithuanian territory. The country recovered from the devastation of war and became a prosperous member of the European community including membership in the League of Nations.

In 1939, Stalin and Hitler entered into a secret pact dividing Eastern Europe into "spheres of influence". This infamous pact allowed Hitler to attack Poland and start the Second World War.

Lithuania fell under the Soviet Union's "sphere of influence" and on June 15, 1940 was occupied along with Latvia and Estonia by the Soviet Union. In July of 1940 a mock election was held "electing" a new parliament based on a single slate of Communist candidates. At that time Lithuanian Communist Party membership was less than one-tenth of one percent of eligible voters.

The new parliament with Red Army bayonets over their heads immediately "voted" for admission to the Soviet Union.

The Russians proceeded to nationalize all private properties and deported over 40,000 people, mostly intellectuals, to Siberia—out of the total population of about three million.

The "friendship" between the two dictators, Hitler and Stalin, did not last long. Nazi Germany attacked the Soviet Union on June 22, 1941 and Lithuania was occupied by the Germans in about four days. When the fortunes of war for Nazi Germany reversed, the Soviet Union reoccupied Lithuania in 1944 and the terror resumed. Lithuanians started a guerilla warfare that lasted until 1953. The fight for freedom cost Lithuanians dearly: about 400,000 dead or deported to Siberia including about 50,000 partisans. After Khrushchev denounced Stalin in the 1950s, some deportees were permitted to return to Lithuania. The return rate was pitiful, for only about 20% of the deportees survived the harsh treatment in Siberia.

WHAT IS HAPPENING NOW?

After guerilla warfare, Lithuanians were disillusioned that the Western powers were not going to come to their rescue, neither militarily nor politically. They have learned how to undermine the occupier's designs by passive resistance and a mild form of sabotage.

With Gorbachev's perestroika and glasnost as the shield, Lithuanians began to show that the will of the people to be free is neither dead nor forgotten. In early 1988 Lithuanians formed "SAJUDIS" (MOVEMENT) in the spirit of perestroika and glasnost. The Movement transcended all political views and the strata of Lithuanian society. A number of Communist Party members were also active members of the Movement. In the middle of 1988 they demanded and got back the symbols of independence: the national anthem, the national flag and the Lithuanian language was declared the official language of the republic, replacing Russian.

In elections on March of 1989, the Lithuanian people soundly trounced the Communist candidates; out of 43 candidates, 42 Movement-backed candidates were elected. Another political push was made regarding economic sovereignty. This was granted by the Supreme Soviet and as of January 1, 1990 Lithuania, Latvia and Estonia acquired rights to manage their economy and natural resources, including the printing of their own currency albeit not convertible into hard currency. Not yet anyway! It is my belief and the belief of economic authorities that the granting of economic sovereignty to the three Baltic States was not a magnanimous gesture but rather an economic necessity for the Soviet Union. The economy of the Soviet Union is in a shambles, in fact, it is on the brink of bankruptcy. Just think, 45 years after the war, sugar and soap are on ration cards. Having the three Baltic States successful economically would serve Gorbachev well; it would be a showcase for perestroika. The liberalization through glasnost and perestroika is sweeping Eastern Europe and what appears to be the unraveling of the Soviet Union itself.

In December, 1989 Lithuanians using this precipitous event, declared their Communist Party independent of Moscow's Central Party and demanded the independence of their country, i.e. secession from the Soviet Union citing the declaration by the Supreme Soviet that the Hitler – Stalin pact of 1939 is illegal. Hence the country was occupied by the Soviet Union illegally in 1940.

Over the last 50 years Lithuanians learned well; one cannot achieve independence with the force of arms against an overwhelming might, but one can win concessions using political methods and exploiting the weakness of the occupier. Gorbachev's well-publicized visit to Lithuania failed to calm down or delay the demands for independence. If anything, it merely accelerated the process. It showed the world that the Lithuanian independence movement is alive and well and is being supported by the overwhelming majority of the people, including, I might add, some of the Russian and other minorities of the country.

The Lithuanian Movement achieved these astonishing results through their representatives in a peaceful and extremely well-disciplined manner. Witness well-behaved crowds in Vilnius and other Lithuanian cities during Gorbachev's visit where he was accorded a statesman's dignity and a polite but strong NO regarding the delay on independence.

WHAT ABOUT THE FUTURE:

Recent events in Eastern Europe and the Soviet Union have happened so swiftly and unexpectedly that the Soviet Union and, to a great extent, other Western countries, were caught by surprise and unprepared to effectively deal with these changes. As usual we are reacting; we have no coherent policy or strategy. In my opinion, the shedding of Communism in Eastern Europe including the unification of Germany will happen whether we like it or not. One thing is certain, the US and other Western economic powers will wind up helping the shattered economies of Eastern Europe including the three Baltic States: Lithuania, Latvia and Estonia. Based on the well-known efficiency, industriousness, self help and organizational ability of the Eastern European countries, we will not see a repeat of the financial fiasco that happened in the Third World.

As for Lithuania and the other Baltic states, independence will come and, I hope, very soon. The delay would be extremely dangerous. Gorbachev's announcement on February 5th regarding the abolishment of the Communist primacy and establishing a multi-party system in the Soviet Union will no doubt be approved by the parliament, but it will create a volatile situation. One must remember that the Soviet Union (Russia) has no experience with a democratic multi-party system of government, save the eight months of the Kerensky government in 1917. The creation of a multi-party system in the Soviet Union could result in anarchy and the breakup of the Soviet Empire; worse: it may invite another dictator.

The breakup of the Soviet Empire would be good for all the oppressed minorities, read <u>RE-PUBLICS</u>, of the USSR. However, I do foresee a civil war and bloodshed. Just recall the recent events in Azerbaijan, Armenia and Georgia; this was child's play compared to what could happen if countries such as the Ukraine, Bielorussia, Kazakhstan and others decide to secede. As far as Lithuania and other Baltic states are concerned, Gorbachev would be crazy to try to hold onto them. To quote a recent Forbes magazine editorial: Why Gorbachev stakes his stack on keeping Lithuania in the USSR is beyond me. Lithuania, Latvia and Estonia, by the Soviets own recent admission, as well as to the world's full knowledge, were illegally annexed by the now-denounced Stalin in his heinous pact with Hitler. With all the massive problems engulfing Comrade Gorbachev, it's hard to see why he is making such an unscalable mountain out of one that should not be".

In conclusion, I foresee the independence of Lithuania, Latvia and Estonia soon, whether by political force or by emergence from anarchy. I foresee the Baltic States becoming democracies and worthy and prosperous members in the community of European countries and partners in the economic well-being of Russia and the Western world.

Ladies and Gentlemen, I thank you for your indulgence.

## H. **Local Lithuanians Watch Developments Anxiously**

By Charles F. Trentelman, Staff Reporter of STANDARD EXAMINER, Ogden, UT, May 13, 1990

Two Lithuanians who live in Utah don't entirely agree what should be done in their native country. Both view it as a volatile situation. But, where one says Lithuanians need to slow down and take it easy, the other says the time to move is now, and criticizes the United States for not taking a stronger stand. Both live in Ogden now. Both got out of Lithuania during World War II when the getting was good.

It was not a good period to be living in that part of the world. Estonia, Latvia and Lithuania had been made independent at the end of World War I, but were small countries easily swept over by the events of World War II.

Put into the Soviet sphere of influence by the Hitler-Stalin pact of 1939, they were occupied by Soviet troops, then occupied by German invaders, then re-occupied by Soviet troops driving the Germans back.

Ursula Mudrow, who works at the local school cafeteria and whose husband runs a printing business in Ogden, was born in 1927 in what was then, the free Republic of Lithuania. She stayed in the country through most of World War II. Her father died in a prison camp in Leningrad during the war and her mother was killed in an Allied air raid in Pomerania. She got out near the end of the war, fleeing west to Germany before the advancing Soviet troops. She came to the United States after the war.

Leon Staciokas, now senior vice president of operations at Iomega, left in 1944 when he was 16 years old. Like most refugees then, he said, he faced a choice between the Nazis and the Soviets. He picked the Nazis because "when you have two evils you choose the lesser one, and at that time the Nazis were the lesser". It was a smart decision, he said – many of his relatives ended up dead or in the Soviet prison camps in Siberia.

Both have since been back – Mudrow three years ago and Staciokas as recently as two months ago, just before the country's March 11 declaration of independence.

Mudrow said it is important to remember that Lithuanians do not and never have considered themselves part of the Soviet Union. They aren't the same kind of people either racially or religiously, she said. Where Soviets are Slavic, the Lithuanians are Baltic. Where Soviets are Russian Orthodox, Lithuanians are Catholic. They don't use the same alphabet or language, and the Lithuanians are culturally more western than the Soviets. "Lithuanians are proud people," Mudrow said. "They have kept their language no matter what through all the different changes".

Staciokas pointed out that many people don't know Lithuania's history. In the 15th century, it was a much larger country, he said. "It stretched from the Baltic to the Black Sea" taking in parts of what are now Poland, White Russia and the Ukraine, then formed a merger with Poland that lasted 300 years until the two were occupied and divided by the Russian, Prussian and Austro-Hungarian empires.

After World War II, he said, the Lithuanians waged an eight year guerrilla war against the Soviets, fighting without aid from other countries. If nothing else, he said, that shows the determination of the people. He said that determination has surfaced recently in the lack of violence in Lithuania, despite what Staciokas sees as blatant Soviet provocations.

"Lithuanians in these trying times have been very, very disciplined," he said. When he was there in March, "the people said the leaders are advising against violence because 3.5 million (the population of Lithuania) versus 280 million (in the Soviet Union), the odds are pretty bad".

## Addendum

It is how Western powers should be reacting to the situation where Mudrow and Staciokas differ, although both agree that the eventual outcome should be independence for the country. Mudrow said her feeling is that the Lithuanians are pushing things too fast. Now a U.S. citizen, she sees danger in the United States becoming directly involved in the dispute. "I think we should stay out of it," she said. "They have to work that out by themselves. That's an internal Russian thing". She said the action of declaring independence and pushing the issue has caused the economic blockade which she doesn't see Lithuania winning. "Right now I really feel sorry for them, but I think they are pushing things. I think they could work it out if they gave it time".

Staciokas feels nothing is going to get worked out unless there is pressure. He said the March 11 declaration was not just a rushed deal – it was calculated to be passed before the Soviet legislature could approve a bill making it much harder to secede. Before that bill was passed, he said, the Soviet Constitution said any member of the union could leave, and that was what Lithuania wanted to do. The Lithuanians felt they even had Gorbachev's tacit approval for the step, since the Soviet government has admitted the Hitler-Stalin pact of 1939, which gave Lithuania to the Soviets, was illegal.

"So we try to declare independence simply by doing what Gorbachev has been saying," he said, but Gorbachev resisted, "so effectively, he (Gorbachev) has stolen goods but is not willing to give them up".

History is repeating itself here, he said. For example, the refusal of foreign countries to act more positively for Lithuania now reminds him of the end of World War II when "the allied leaders didn't want to rattle the cages of Stalin" and force him to take his troops out of Eastern Europe. "We sacrifice small countries for the sake of getting along" he said. "This is what's happening now. The U.S. agenda is to get the Russians economic assistance and also to some extent to get the weapons agreements, missile agreements, and I think these are all worthwhile endeavors but here again I think Gorbachev is talking from weakness and blustering because he has no resources to sustain a military establishment for a long time"

Then there is the insistence by Gorbachev that no violence will be used, he said. "I don't know what you call it when the tanks roll through the city and they invade hospitals and newspaper printing facilities," he said.

306

# I. Lithuanian Warns of Machiavellian Gorbachev
## By Karen Cobb, Staff writer of the Signpost

The Honors Issues Forum and the International Forum hosted Lithuanian-born Leon Staciokas at Thursday's Open Hour. Staciokas presented the facts and his views concerning the impending problems faced by Lithuania and USSR.

Staciokas described Gorbachev as a very dangerous leader and the most Machiavellian in this century. "Passing laws is one thing," said Staciokas, "but enforcing them is another, especially with the KGB and the Red Army around the corner".

Staciokas made this comment about Gorbachev who he feels says one thing while doing another. Gorbachev, according to Staciokas, has also made continuous contradictions on defense, the economy and relations with other countries.

One of the contradictions Gorbachev has made concerns the Baltic States. In 1988 he said that if the Baltic States, or any other state, including Lithuania, wanted to secede, they could. Today he is firmly saying NO to secession.

In 1795 Lithuania became part of the tsarist Russian empire. At the end of WWI in 1918, Lithuania declared independence and proclaimed itself a democratic republic. In 1920 they signed a peace treaty with Russia which renounced all rights to the Lithuanian territory.

In 1939, Stalin and Hitler formed the pact "spheres of influence" resulting in Lithuania succumbing to Russian rule again. A mock election was held based on single slate of Communist candidates. The Russians proceeded to nationalize all private properties and 40,000 people were deported to Siberia. The Lithuanian way of life came basically to a halt with wide spread persecution. For example, "Forty Catholic churches were in existence," said Staciokas, "in 1985 there were only two".

Staciokas believes that glasnost and perestroika is what brought the Lithuanian people out of the woodwork. "Lithuanians are showing the world their will to be free," said Staciokas. In 1988, Lithuanians formed "SAJUDIS" or Movement as a support group to continue the determination for Lithuanian freedom.

Although Lithuanians are under much strain, Staciokas said the people are very disciplined. "No one is rioting or giving cause for provocations," said Staciokas, "and they are not intimidated by the Soviet military power".

Lithuanians will continue to exist, "Notice I said exist, not live," he said. "People are simply surviving there". Basic survival and the hope for freedom are keeping Lithuanians abreast. Lithuania has no natural resources but has a strong agricultural economy.

A woman said to Staciokas on his recent visit to Lithuania in March, "We are running out of oil, but we can use wood stoves, we'll be okay. I just wonder what Muscovites will do without the food we usually give them".

"I believe the upcoming summit with Bush and Gorbachev will only be window dressing instead of reality," said Staciokas.

Gorbachev needs economic assistance from the US said Staciokas. Therefore, he does not foresee Gorbachev imposing presidential rule because it would mean military occupation and martial law. However, Staciokas does predict independence for Lithuania because sooner or later Gorbachev will have to come to truth with the fact that Lithuania was illegally annexed by "the now denounced Stalin in his heinous pact with Hitler".

NOTE: Printed in "SIGNPOST" newspaper on May 25, 1990. This is a newspaper shared by three or four Utah state universities.

**J. Lithuania – Past, Present and Future**
**Presented to Weber State University**
**By Leon Staciokas**
**March 7, 1991**

INTRODUCTION:
Lithuania has a long history. In the 14th and 15th centuries, Lithuania was the most powerful country in Eastern Europe. In the 16th century, Lithuania formed a union (Commonwealth) with Poland which lasted about 300 years. Corruption in government, oppression of the peasants and the suicidal veto power in parliament resulted in the demise of the country. By the end of the 18th century, the Union was partitioned by Prussia, Russia and Austro-Hungary. Most of today's Lithuanian territory was occupied by Russia.

LITHUANIAN HISTORY IN THE TWEN-
TIETH CENTURY
After the First World War, in 1918, Lithu-ania restored its independence which lasted until 1940. In August, 1939 the Soviet Union in collu-sion with Nazi Germany divided Poland, Lithu-ania, Latvia and Estonia into spheres of influence. In June, 1940 Lithuania was occupied by the So-viet Union and forcibly incorporated as one of the Soviet republics. At the latter part of June, 1941

Lithuania fell to Nazi Germany as a result of the USSR war with Germany. In 1944, with the retreat of the Nazis, Lithuania was reoccupied by the Soviet Union. For eight years, from 1945 to 1953, Lithuanians waged guerrilla warfare without any support from the outside democratic world. In the end, the result of this uneven battle was about 60,000 guerrillas killed or captured, out of the total population of about three million. Lithuanians paid a terrible price for the resistance to Communism: approximately 300,000 (10%) of the people were deported to Siberia; about 100,000 escaped to the West; all private property was expropriated without compensation and the Soviets attempted to deprive the people of Lithuanian culture and heritage. These travails and vicissitudes of Lithuania lasted from 1940 to 1988.

RECENT EVENTS

Before mid 1988, the name Lithuania meant very little or nothing to most of the Western World including the United States. Late in 1988 the Lithuanians using glasnost and perestroika, began to voice their desires to regain what was lost in 1939. At first timidly, then more forcefully they began to demand acknowledgement from the Kremlin that this small nation, next to the Baltic Sea, was alive and deserved its independence. Slowly the symbols of independent Lithuania were being restored: the national flag, the national anthem, the celebration of the Independence Day and many other signs of independence signaled the people's desire for freedom.

During 1989, the quest for freedom accelerated; the newspapers that were prohibited for almost 50 years began to be published. The contents of these papers spoke eloquently about independence. The television programs were echoing the independence movement. During 1989, the news media began to speak of the atrocities committed under Stalin, such as the number of people deported to Siberia, where they had to live in the most inhuman conditions, the tortures inflicted to those that were arrested; and most of these stories were told by the survivors of these atrocities. Traveling through Lithuania in the summer of 1989, you felt you were no longer in the Soviet Union; the smiling faces, the pride of people spoke eloquently of their newly found freedom.

In the last quarter of 1989, the Lithuanian Communist Party, albeit small in numbers, split from Moscow. The reason given by the Lithuanian Communist Party leadership was that they would lose very badly in the forthcoming free elections (first in 50 years).

The movement for independence was so

strong that it worried Gorbachev greatly. In January, 1990, Gorbachev came to Lithuania to convince the Lithuanian leadership and the people on the street to remain in the Soviet Union. During this visit he was accorded the courtesy as the head of state, but was told firmly in spite of his threats and blustering that Lithuania intended to seek its independence.

In February 1990, the election for the parliament was held with the overwhelming election of candidates from the "Sąjudis" (Movement). Sąjudis was an association of independence minded people irrespective of their political leanings. On March 11, 1990, the new democratically elected parliament declared the restoration of Lithuanian independence.

I was in Lithuania between March 1-6, 1990 and it was common knowledge about the parliament intentions. Euphoria was tempered with somber assessment of the situation; the large military contingent was in the country, the economic life was interwoven with the USSR, the key industries such as transportation and energy were in the Soviet hands, and the Kremlin's resistance to independence was an impediment. But the determination of the people was there.

The patience and discipline of people was tried sorely when Moscow imposed economic sanctions in the spring of 1990. In spite of economic hardships, the people of Lithuania did not give up. By this time the world's opinion began to question Gorbachev's glasnost and perestroika; was it a reality or a mirage?

The events in Kuwait in August 1990 severely restricted the true expression of the sympathies of the US government, who was trying to form an effective coalition in the Persian Gulf to eject Iraq from Kuwait. Unfortunately the Soviet Union was needed in this coalition.

The year of 1990 exposed the true economic situation in the Soviet Union for the entire world to see. The internal disarray within the Soviet Union and even within the Kremlin ruling gang was causing severe economic hardships to the Soviet people. Gorbachev began to rely more and more on the military and the KGB. The reformers were removed or resigned from their positions of power and were replaced with the old hard line Stalinist communists. The glasnost and perestroika were thrown away into the heap of political failures.

What does this mean to Lithuania? The recent events and the behavior of Gorbachev would appear to doom the independence drive. The bloody Sunday of January, where 14 people were killed and over 150 injured, when the Soviet troops

stormed the television station in Vilnius only ac-
centuated what it means to tangle with the Russian
bear. The order to attack and kill unarmed civilians was issued by Gorbachev, the man that received the Nobel Peace Prize. To put this carnage
into perspective, if the same number of casualties, based on population size, were suffered by the
US forces in the Persian Gulf, the total killed and
wounded in the US would have been over 15,000
instead of a few hundred.

The intimidation and threats from the Kremlin
towards Lithuania is increasing. The recent referendum in Lithuania shows that over 90% voted
for independence. Over 96% of eligible voters
cast ballots. Even the minorities, (about 20% of
the total population) voted overwhelmingly for independence.

The same type of referendum in the other
two Baltic countries, Latvia and Estonia was held
on March 3rd with comparable results to those of
Lithuania. In spite of an overwhelming mandate,
Gorbachev asserts that these referendums are illegal and have no constitutional basis. Technically
he is correct but morally, in the eyes of the free
world, he is wrong.

The referendum that will take place on March
17th throughout the Soviet Union is designed to
preserve the crumbling Soviet Empire and assure

the top job for Gorbachev. The wording of the referendum is such that it makes it very difficult to vote NO. The wording: "Should the Soviet Union of Federated Sovereign Republics be preserved with equal rights for all ethnic groups in the Union".

The problem is that the current constitution, as modified by Gorbachev and ratified by parliament (not totally democratically elected), have no words or phrases explaining the FEDERATION and SOVEREIGN states. The interpretation of those words in Russian has several meanings. In essence, Gorbachev is "putting the cart before the horse". If his referendum was based on good intentions (which it is not), it should have been prepared on the premise of a totally new constitution which defines the FEDERATION and SOVEREIGNTY and then asks people to vote for or against it. In any case, the outcome of the referendum is not a certainty; it will greatly depend on the position of Boris Yeltsin. He is very popular in the Russian and some other Soviet Republics. If he decides to oppose the referendum, it would not pass. The three Baltic Republics, Lithuania, Latvia and Estonia as well as Georgia and Moldavian Republics already stated that they will boycott the referendum.

Currently with the miners' strike spreading,

with a more unified voice of the various democratic movements in the Soviet Union opposing the Kremlin, with the economy getting worse every day and the drive for independence of the Baltic States, the situation is very tenuous bordering on anarchy. Gorbachev is no longer capable of providing leadership because he has lost the confidence of his former associates who helped him to promulgate glasnost and perestroika and he has lost the confidence of the people.

THE FUTURE:

In view of the current situation in the Soviet Union, what is the status of Lithuania now and what might be the future for the country?

1. The present situation is very uncertain and if the past behavior of Gorbachev is any indicator, anything can happen any time. One thing is for certain, Gorbachev will not allow Lithuania to become independent unless the pressure from the US and the European Common Market will force him to permit the Baltic States independence in return for an economic bailout of the Soviet Union.

   There is a reasonable likelihood of anarchy and a possible civil war after the referendum on March 17th, no matter what the outcome will be of that referendum. The negative vote would merely accelerate the process.

2. There is also a good possibility of total economic collapse in 1991 in which case some republics will go their separate ways with some upheavals, but not total civil war. In this scenario the behavior of the Russian Republic and Boris Yeltsin will be an important factor.

3. There might be a return of the hardliners similar to the Stalin days, but this would only be temporary. The democratic forces have enough influence to overcome such a situation.

4. There is also a possibility of a military coup, but this would not last long for the same reason as the hardliners scenario. Besides, there is no noted military man of statue that could govern the country. The military is discredited with very low morale.

The working and living conditions of the democratically elected Lithuanian government is deplorable. The parliament building is barricaded, a number of parliamentarians including the president of the Lithuanian Republic sleep in the building. Several government buildings are occupied by the Red Army troops, the Interior Department has a Moscow appointed interior minister with no duties and no staff (Lithuanians refuse to work with him). It is a modern day miracle that the government functions as efficiently as it does. There is constant threat of Gorbachev's presidential rule; the newspapers are being deprived of printing presses that are controlled by the Red Army troops.

The economy is just a little bit better than in the Soviet Union at large, primarily the food supplies. Such is Gorbachev's glasnost and perestroika as it really is, not as the Western World including the United States wishes it to be. This is the daily life in Lithuania today.

Out of all this confusion, I foresee Lithuania gaining independence no later than in the fall of 1991 or early in 1992. Under any circumstances, the country is facing a very difficult future for the next five years, especially economic difficulties.

When I think about Lithuania's future, I am reminded of the passage in the Russian writer Gogol's "Dead Souls". Comparing the nation to a speeding troika (three horses hitched to a wagon) Gogol asks what will be its destination. And he writes: "There is no answer save the bells pouring forth marvelous sound".

In the current situation, the Lithuanian people and the government displayed remarkable discipline and restraint. They can make the country succeed but it will need both economic and moral support from the United States and other Western countries.

WILL THAT SUPPORT COME?

Made in the USA
Columbia, SC
20 January 2024

30721037R00183